THE R PLAYBOOK

HOW TO INCREASE SALES WITH PROVEN NETWORKING STRATEGIES

"Take your networking game to the next level with this book."

Foreword by
Dr. Ivan Misner
Founder and Chief Visionary Officer
BNI-Business Network International

By Rick Itzkowich

The Referral Playbook
*How to Increase Sales with
Proven Networking Strategies*
by **Rick Itzkowich**

Copyright © 2018 Rick Itzkowich
Published by SkillBites LLC
All rights reserved.

No part of this book may be reproduced or transmitted in any form or by any means whatsoever without written permission from the author, except in the case of brief quotations embodied in critical articles and reviews.

DISCLAIMER AND/OR LEGAL NOTICES

While the publisher and author have used their best efforts in preparing this book, they make no representations or warranties with respect to the accuracy or completeness of the contents of this book. The advice and strategies contained herein may not be suitable for your situation. You should consult a professional where appropriate. Neither the publisher nor the author shall be liable for any loss of profit or any other commercial damages, including but not limited to special, incidental, consequential, or other damages. The purchaser or reader of this publication assumes responsibility for the use of these materials and information. Adherence to all applicable laws and regulations, both advertising and all other aspects of doing business in the United States or any other jurisdiction, is the sole responsibility of the purchaser or reader.

ISBN-10: 1-942489-59-5
ISBN-13: 978-1-942489-59-7

TESTIMONIALS

"Well done! You've identified an unforgiving gap—the gap between networking activities and actual lead generation. Everyone is told to do online and face-to-face networking to generate leads. But, when push comes to shove, how does one convert these leads to profits? In the playbook you've provided a step-by-step process. The bonus is you've covered a lot of important information without the book being too long."

Lindon Crow
Founder/Owner
Productive Learning

"*The Referral Playbook* is a golden nugget. I love that you go into the success mindset and share your formulas for success. It's the ideal length too. A+ on making more deposits before withdrawals. When networking, many people walk around handing out their cards, showing no real interest in others. When you get into the game plays, you make metrics easy to understand, even for non-numbers people. The playbook puts it all together in an easy way to monetize success. There are lots of great coaching ideas to help a business owner or salesperson play the game to win!"

Kathy Nelson, CPPC, RScP
Life & Business Coach
On Track Success Coaching

"I have read hundreds of business books and the vast majority have several valuable points that can be summed up in an eight-page executive summary. *The Referral Playbook* is insightful, valuable and powerful. Packed within its pages are many, many valuable tips, techniques, tutorials and resources for both the novice and the veteran sales professional. If you are ready to get serious about sales and referrals, order this book today."

Alan Sorkin
Master Vistage Chair, Vistage Worldwide
CEO, Premier Asset Management Services, Inc.

"As an engineer, I've succeeded in sales thanks to having an effective sales process. The same is not true for my networking activities. Your book gave me practical and actionable ideas that I have turned into an effective networking process."

Mitch Gooze
Principal
Customer Manufacturing Group, Inc.

"As a busy CPA, I have to make sure that the time I spend at networking events is worth my while. In the playbook, you provide an insider-secret formula I use to add people I meet to my database. With their permission, I stay in touch with them using an automated daily email message they absolutely love. It's all explained in the book."

Jeanne Mann, CPA
Founder
Mann & Associates A P.C.

"If I were to train Vistage Chairs on how to launch or grow their groups, I would require them to read this book. It is a quick and easy read filled with practical tools and tactics. It's also worth rereading and revisiting this book at many points in your Vistage Chair journey."

Adam Harris
Director
Fresh Mindset UK Ltd.

"Just read *The Referral Playbook* end-to-end, and I say it is outstanding. This is a must read for anyone looking for a practical way to generate more referrals."

Thomas Gay
CEO-Chairman & Founder
Refer.com

"I love this book — well done! If one is interested in converting their lead generation and referrals into money in the bank, this short read is the way to do it. It truly is a playbook — concise, practical, and step-by-step. Now I have quite a few more strategies to consider doing for myself and my BNI business. I thank you for that!"

Susan Goodsell
Executive Director
BNI Riverside & San Bernardino, California

"This is a great book for anyone wanting to initiate or recharge their personal branding process. *The Referral Playbook* does a nice job in separating lead generation and selling from networking."

Mark Fingerlin
Chair, Vistage Worldwide
CEO, Northstar Advisors, Inc.

"As a marketing consultant, I look to making your book required reading for new clients. Rather than just boring theory, you give how-to examples and hands-on resources for solo-preneurs and sales teams to use in their day-to-day activities. The playbook also gets across the 'why' and the 'how' to make face-to-face networking pay off. If a person implements just one-tenth of the action items you recommend, they will see their sales results magnified ten-fold."

Susan Almon-Pesch, CME, CMC
Owner
Market 4 Profit

"The book was outstanding. Simple, not too complex, yet gives the details so that the reader can actually 'take action.' Now I am getting to work!"

Mike Malone
Vistage Chair

"You have taken concepts like BNI's 'Givers Gain' and strategies like inviting people to connect on LinkedIn and given me a cohesive game plan on how to leverage the concepts and action items for measurable results. I will no longer do random networking or isolated gift giving. After reading *The Referral Playbook*, I've got this!"

Christie Kramer-LeVander
REALTOR® BRE # 00902753
Sea Coast Exclusive Properties

DEDICATION

It is with gratitude and love that I dedicate this book to my late father, Moises Itzkowich and my mother, Norma Armon. I am who I am today thanks to your support, guidance, encouragement, and the example you set for me.

DONATION

In honor of my father, Moises Itzkowich, 100% of the proceeds from The Referral Playbook, print and ebook versions, will go to the Alzheimer's Foundation of America. My dad passed away January 2018 after braving the battle of Alzheimer's.

The Alzheimer's Foundation of America (AFA) was founded by a consortium of organizations to fill the gap that existed on a national level to assure quality of care and excellence in service to individuals with Alzheimer's disease and related illnesses, and to their caregivers and families. AFA's mission is to provide optimal care and services to individuals confronting dementia, and to their caregivers and families - through member organizations dedicated to improving quality of life.

For more information, visit AFA at https://alzfdn.org

ACKNOWLEDGMENTS

It would take paragraphs upon paragraphs to thank everyone who has encouraged and supported me over the years. In the space I have, I want to be sure to mention Ivan Misner, Ph.D., Lindon Crow, Susan Almon-Pesch, Judy Weintraub, and my Inner Circle tribe of supporters. Ivan, because he so graciously reviewed my book draft and contributed the Foreword. Dr. Misner is called the "Father of Modern Networking" by CNN and the "Networking Guru" by *Entrepreneur* magazine. He is recognized as one of the world's leading experts on business networking. Lindon, because he is my sounding board and was my partner in my first company Productive Learning & Leisure (now Productive Learning). Susan, because she helps me market and implement my ideas—turning them into products and services. Judy, because her company, SkillBites LLC diligently worked with me to edit and publish *The Referral Playbook*. And last, but by far, not the least, my Inner Circle of family, friends, clients, connections, colleagues and more. The success I have experienced is due in large part to their confidence in my coaching, articles, products and services. Thank you all for your encouragement and support.

FOREWORD

The global business community is recognizing the value of simplification. Our bandwidth for adding more ways to sell and get referrals is too low. In *The Referral Playbook: How to Increase Sales with Proven Networking Strategies,* Rick Itzkowich has identified how to combine time-honored networking and innovative online strategies in an easy-to-follow simplified guide.

Rick is a genuine people connector. He bridges the two worlds of face-to-face networking and online networking. He is an authority on this subject because he's lived it for more than 25 years. As the CEO of a successful manufacturing company and former business partner of a professional development firm, Rick has logged more than 30,000 hours of corporate facilitation. Today as owner of 501 Connections, a San Diego-based business, networking, and referrals coaching company and Vistage Chair, he helps CEOs exponentially increase their company's growth rate.

Rick served as President of the award-winning BNI Del Mar Chapter three terms over 18 years. I've watched Rick increase his business ten-fold through a structured, positive and professional referral marketing program using the BNI Givers Gain® philosophy. He was my guest in 2010 for my BNI Podcast Episode 146: Visibility Through Touchpoints. Listen at http://ntwrk.biz/qabnipod

In *The Referral Playbook,* Rick set out to give networking newbies and veterans a step-by-step guide for making networking translate into business. The systems and processes he shares in this playbook are scalable. He's shown by incorporating simple metrics, one can ramp up or slow down the process and methods of action as needed to turn referrals into customers for life.

If you are an entrepreneur, small business owner, sales leader or salesperson looking for help creating ways to stay top-of-mind, so when your networking referrals and prospects are ready to buy they think of you, then this is the book for you.

If you found this book because you've never committed to weekly face-to-face networking and are struggling to see how it fits in your sales process, this book will give you the tried and proven answers.

I believe if you follow the plays Rick has laid out—from embracing the right networking mindset all the way through applying simple sales ratio formulas for your day-to-day sales actions, your business revenues will improve exponentially.

I would recommend the *The Referral Playbook* to individuals serious about taking their online and offline networking game to the next level. Like an all-star coach Rick has designed a game plan to help you develop and nurture long-term, meaningful relationships that will lead to more business.

Dr. Ivan Misner
Founder and Chief Visionary Officer

BNI-Business Network International
Best Selling Author
- *Healing Begins in the Kitchen: Get Well and Stay There with the Misner Plan*
- *Masters of Networking*
- *Networking Like a Pro: Turning Contacts into Connections*
- *The 29% Solution: 52 Weekly Networking Success Strategies*

CONTENTS

Testimonials 3

Dedication 6

Acknowledgments 7

Foreword 8

My Story 11

Why a Playbook? 17

Getting Your Game On 19

Quality Equipment to Win 32

Game Strategies 60

Four Key Game Components 70

Putting Your Game Plan Together 77

What About? 93

Now What? 125

About the Author 127

Products & Services 129

Thank You Very Much! 132

MY STORY

RICK ITZKOWICH
Vistage Chair, Entrepreneur, Speaker & Author

I come from a family of entrepreneurs. The entrepreneurial bug entered my genes from my grandfather, who came from Europe to Mexico with nothing and built a substantial set of businesses; it was passed on through my father, who grew a small manufacturing operation into a multi-million-dollar success. On the flipside, my mother is a university professor. I have both business and education genes in my DNA. I knew I didn't want to be just a business owner or just an educator, because I like being both.

Over the years, I've forged paths using the gifts I was given. From my self-development company that combined sports and learning to my position as a Vistage Chair and my company 501 Connections that combines online and offline networking with innovative products and services, I am living my dream to help others.

The reason I wrote *The Referral Playbook: How to Increase Sales with Proven Networking Strategies* is that, after being involved in networking for nearly twenty years, I've found huge gaps in the information people need to make optimal use of all the networking options people have, from face-to-face (F2F) networking organizations like BNI and chambers of commerce, to the online business platform LinkedIn. While groups and platforms can coexist, they don't give you step-by-step instructions for making networking successful. Granted, organizations do provide training on how to operate within their parameters, yet I've found no guidance regarding what to do after making connections or how to integrate the online and offline worlds.

I struggled for years. The only way I could get more results from my networking activities was to put in more hours. That formula was not scalable. Furthermore, when it came time to train other people to use networking as a viable option for business development, I didn't have an action plan.

I had no translation from concepts into actionable lead generation steps that could be monitored, managed, and ultimately proven to be working or not. Most people end up having to work harder than they need to—getting a fraction of the results possible—or they get totally discouraged and stop networking altogether. I saw the same thing when I looked into the LinkedIn piece of the networking puzzle. Since people didn't understand it, they just mirrored some of the activities they used in face-to-face networking. This playbook is designed to be a guide for networking newbies and veterans who want to find ways to scale their activities. It is also a viable guide for sales managers to use to train their teams on productive, revenue-producing networking.

IN THE BEGINNING

To write this book, I compiled all my activities and experience with F2F networking through my more than eighteen years with Business Network International (BNI) and the twelve years I've used LinkedIn. I deconstructed the activities and put them back together using reverse engineering.

This culminated when I became a Vistage Chair and my number one job was to launch my peer advisory group. When I put together my business plan, I included networking, and quickly realized there were many gaps that needed to be filled. It's an organic process. I saw there was a need for a system or a process, and I went looking for it in the marketplace. But it didn't exist, and because of that, I created it—*The Referral Playbook: How to Increase Sales with Proven Networking Strategies.*

This playbook is for people who attend networking events, use referral tools, and see the value of building relationships—but don't have a game plan that they can ramp up or slow down as needed to turn referrals into business. By using the strategies and "plays" in this book, you will be able to speed up the sales process when you need more prospects or slow it down when you have too many—without ever losing what you have achieved.

PRODUCTS WITH A PURPOSE

Throughout this playbook, I refer to products and services I've used. Why reinvent the wheel? When I train people, I tell them to use these products and services instead of going out and rediscovering them on their own. By no means are these the only products or services that are available to do the job. The approximate costs I mention for the products and services included in the book are based on current 2018 pricing.

I'm proud to say I created some of these products and services because there was a demand. If there wasn't anything doing what I needed it to do, I went about creating a product. Since then, some other products may have been developed to do the same thing, but I'm partial to my products as they were designed to fit into my tried and proven lead generation system.

QUOTEACTIONS

One of these products is QuoteActions. I developed QuoteActions during the recession in 2007, when I had a self-development business. I saw a trend in my newsletters. The cost of production—first in the print newsletters, then the email newsletters—was going up, and the readership was going down.

I wanted a way to stay in frequent contact with my clients and prospects that was cost-effective and would add value. At the time, my former business partner would write some articles; I saw that those articles were the ones the readers enjoyed the most. What if we could have an article delivered to people every day? That quickly proved to be a nonstarter. But I kept pressing the whole concept. I ended up with the idea of delivering quotes—motivational, inspirational quotes. I personally like them and had frequently used them in my communications.

I searched the internet and nothing was available that didn't include advertising for someone else. The idea to make the quotes actionable, to bring the quotes to life, was born. My personal development company combined positive-living concepts with sports and adventure travel. It was all about giving people information through actions.

At first, we delivered the QuoteActions by phone. One client called me and said they loved my QuoteActions because they thought of me each time they received one. They wanted to use them with their own clients. That's all it took for me to launch a new business. I changed up the delivery to email, and today QuoteActions is a visibility product used by thousands of companies to stay at the top of their clients' and prospects' minds.

LINK POWER NOW

My Link Power Now (LPN) product was developed because people were asking me for help with LinkedIn. I had jumped on the LinkedIn platform when it first came out. I spent hundreds of hours researching how to use it: the best practices, the etiquette of the portal, and more. I learned how to make LinkedIn more than an online place to park one's resume. People would hear about the success I was having getting referrals and recommendations, and they would ask me to show them how. I became "Rick I., The LinkedIn Guy." Quite frankly, I didn't have the bandwidth or the time to help as many people as I wanted to, so I made video recordings to give people direction. One day someone called and asked, "Hey Rick, I'd like to buy your videos." I chimed back, "what videos?" He said, "The ones my friends tell me about. They say you're the LinkedIn Guy, and you have these videos on how to use LinkedIn." Like QuoteActions, Link Power Now has taken off and is ordered around the world.

ROCK-IT! REFERRALS

The Rock-It! Referrals (RIR) system is another product I developed out of a need. Once again, the methodology came to me by accident. During my weekly BNI meeting, I asked my colleagues for introductions to CEOs for the launch of my Vistage peer advisory group. Many said they would. A week later, I still hadn't gotten a single introduction. After the meeting, I had a one-on-one appointment with a member. I mentioned that she had said she would have some introductions to CEOs for me. She apologized profusely and said quite frankly that she had totally dropped the ball. Out of the blue, I had an idea. I had my laptop, and I said "let's log in to your LinkedIn account right now." After a quick search of her connections using the CEO filter, within 15 minutes she had given me five introductions to ideal CEO referrals. That's when it dawned on me—people are willing to help you if you make it easy for them and provide them with the tools. I went on to create the Rock-It! Referrals product to make it easy for others to give referrals in this same manner.

MY GOAL

In short, I didn't set out to create products for money. I developed solutions to problems I was facing. It just so happens that I knew the products that emerged would be valuable to other people. Since 2007, I've sold more than a million dollars' worth of products to thousands of people. Just imagine the business dollars that have been generated!

My goal is to help businesspeople bridge the two worlds of face-to-face and online networking for lead generation success. If you've come across this book, you're most likely searching for a next-generation mindset and step-by-step guide to propel your business growth. I hope you will embrace the concepts and the actions you find here in *The Referral Playbook*.

In addition, please visit my website https://www.rickitzkowich.com often to read articles, watch videos, and learn about my new books, products and services.

WHY A PLAYBOOK?

There has been a gap—a significant gap—between networking and lead generation activities and generating sales.

Enter The Referral Playbook: How to Increase Sales with Proven Networking Strategies!

This playbook is for business owners, business development staff, marketing teams, sales managers, sales agents, sales reps—as well as their administrative assistants.

This book will teach you how to scale your sales and referrals when you want them.

In my work with CEOs, I have found that one of their challenges is having a business development process for lead generation as well as a sales funnel process for conversions. These CEOs and the people working with them realize that they need to build relationships, attend networking events, and convert those connections into sales.

Often, they have many books about these subjects but still haven't taught themselves how to start generating referrals for short- and long-term results. They are not alone as they wonder, "How do I manage to stay in touch with these contacts in a way that is both time-efficient, cost-effective, and that will lead to sales now and in the future?"

This book is designed to help you decrease your networking activities while increasing your referrals with a PROVEN process and methodology.

From CEOs to sales reps to personal business owners, a chief complaint is that they do not have enough time to pull more than one or two conversion tools together. Or they have purchased tools but are worried they've wasted their money. This book is designed to take those areas and bring them together in a cohesive approach for generating more business and sales through this "playbook" process.

In the game of golf, you do not use the same club for every shot. The reason you have fourteen clubs in your bag is because each one of those clubs is designed for a specific purpose. You may find in your day-to-day networking actions that you have your bread-and-butter clubs. However, the more plays you have, the more use you can get from the clubs in your bag.

Some shots call for short distances with a high trajectory. Others require low and long drives, and still others something in-between. Even the club face is designed to do different things: though you may use the same swing, different club faces give you different results.

Likewise, the plays in *The Referral Playbook* are designed to have different results for different circumstances in your sales game.

Let's get your game on!

GETTING YOUR GAME ON

Let's start by getting into the right mindset to play the game of sales and referrals as it relates to how you approach the people around you in networking and relationships.

VALUE IN NETWORKING

First, how do you view networking?

In my twenty-five years of active networking, I've seen that, when people go to networking events or when they practice networking, they focus on volume and on meeting as many people as they can.

Is this what you are doing?

Most do this based on the notion that sooner or later, they will run into the right people to get sales or referrals. The people who practice this way long enough finally understand (either through studying it or from experience) that this mindset is not particularly effective. Networking is different from selling. Networking is not a numbers game—though numbers play a part in the process.

The right mindset going into networking is to intend to be of value to the people with whom you are networking.

This paradigm flip allows you to look at connecting from the perspective of the other people who are also networking. If you can become a significant person to another individual because you offer some value and have generated goodwill, the odds improve considerably that the other person will then feel the need to reciprocate.

For the most part, as human beings, we have connectivity wired into us. If people are nice to us and do things for us, we feel reciprocation is in order. We intrinsically want to do something nice for them.

If you start out with this concept, you will have a positive mindset that will also increase your sales potential.

This process is not always a direct "I'll do this for you, you'll do that for me."

We know as adults that life doesn't happen that way. But if you look at this approach in the aggregate, the harvest may come in from somewhere entirely different than where you planted seeds.

This mindset allows you to grasp the concept more easily and avoid saying, "Yeah, I've done this and this and this for all these other people, and I've yet to see anything come back to me."

My response to those individuals is, "Well, it's not always linear. It doesn't always come back the same way." And in fact, the referral process works better in this manner because not everyone is a good match for you.

Example

I know a fantastic executive recruiter who, in his position, often sees people who are in the job market and need an updated LinkedIn profile. As a result, he often refers people to me. The positions he recruits for are high-end placements, and I really am not in a circle where I run into many of the companies or people who are influential at those companies that would allow me to do a reciprocal referral.

Nonetheless, I feel a need to reciprocate in whatever ways that I can. While I haven't been able to reciprocate with referrals, I've been able to reciprocate in other ways—by giving him information and helping some of his connections.

On the flip side...

I've provided many referrals to another colleague who owns a company that does marketing and public relations. Many of the people whom I work with are small business owners who desperately need her company's help. So, I regularly refer business to her. She has yet to send me any referrals, but nonetheless, she is still of great value to me because I can—with confidence—refer people to her, knowing they're going to be in good hands.

The benefit I get from this scenario is the positive feedback from people who love her services. Thus, I become trustworthy based on my recommendation of her to them.

Remember, reciprocation is not always in the form of one-to-one referrals.

The mindset here is one that starts out with grasping the principle that if you become of value to the people in your network, they will have a desire to help you in return.

NETWORKING PARADIGM SHIFT

With this mindset, the paradigm shifts. Instead of going to networking events for the purpose of finding people who can refer business to you or do business with you, you network from the point of view of having a more powerful network that you can refer among.

You become the gatekeeper. As my network grows not only in quantity but in diversity, I become the go-to person. More people come to me and say, "Hey, Rick. I need this. Who do you know that can help me with that?" Every time someone contacts me, it positions me as a **trusted advisor**. It gives me the opportunity to generate goodwill and enhances the odds that two or more people will now feel "indebted to me" and want to go out of their way to reciprocate.

By being a connector, you will become a trusted advisor.

Networking enables you to be a trusted, knowledgeable, and influential person.

To do this, you need influence. And influence is found by being of service and by adding value to others.

If you're not getting the referrals or the quantity/quality of the referrals you want, ask yourself these questions:

1. How much value have I brought to my network?

For example, have you sent out informational articles or referred trusted advisors to your contacts?

2. How easy have I made it for others to reciprocate to me?

For example, you could include your telephone number on your LinkedIn profile page, provide people with a copy of a brief introduction they can use when they have a referral for you, or use a Refer.com card. Think about the ease (or lack thereof) that your contacts have in giving back to you.

3. Do people know exactly what I do?

If they know what you do, it's easier for them to share you as a contact who can solve a specific problem. For example, I know a business attorney who has told me he specializes in "partnerships." Because he's told me this, I immediately think of him when I hear that someone needs help with a partnership agreement.

4. Have I made myself easy to find?

For example, when someone does a search online for your name, do all your listings readily come up? Everything from LinkedIn, your website, Refer.com, networking groups, testimonials/reviews you've given that are picked up on other websites, and more make you easier to find. We will discuss tools and techniques later, but your answers here may open your eyes to ways your network can expand.

THE LONG-TERM APPROACH

Let's analyze some metaphors to get our minds thinking in the most productive ways about our network.

Farming vs. Hunting

One analogy that is helpful in preparing our minds is to think of networking as farming rather than hunting. Depending on what

you've planted, you may not see any fruits to harvest for several months to years. When we compare farming to hunting, we see a long-term approach rather than a short-term approach. Anytime you hunt for something, you are looking for an immediate result from your actions. Let's apply this mindset to networking. **Are you farming or hunting?** When you focus on farming, you won't have immediate results, but you will have sown many seeds.

Real Estate Developer

Another approach is to think of yourself as a developer who is going to build up a piece of land. Way before the homes are built, long before the golf course is ready, you have to have all the infrastructure in place so that the piece of land becomes more valuable and ready to build out. It's the same approach in networking. You have to build the pieces. You have to build the infrastructure and make it ready so that down the road, you can reap the benefits.

EMBRACE TECHNOLOGY

Technology is a means to an end—not an end in itself. New technologies emerge all the time, and they can be totally overwhelming. But there are certain aspects of technology that allow us to advance in our networking.

Smartphones

Most people in the United States, and increasingly around the world, have a cell phone or access to a cell phone. Imagine being in business today without a smartphone. You wouldn't be taken seriously. Productivity and social media apps provide you with direct connections to your prospects and contacts at all times.

An example would be using your cell phone to send an immediate referral instead of having to go back to your office and send an email introduction.

When you're at a convention, it may be days or weeks before you make the time to follow up with contacts. By continuing to learn what tools are available to you through your phone, tablet, and laptop, you'll enjoy the speed and convenience of networking in today's business world. Following up on a lead immediately will help a relationship bud rather than risking it wither because too much time has passed.

Dump AOL

It's the same with email. Your technology doesn't have to be the latest and greatest, but there are some pieces of technology that are essential. Email is one of them. Make sure your email address reflects the twenty-first century—using your company's URL domain extension versus aol.com or yahoo.com, etc.

Database Management Cloud Software

Database technology services allow us to replace the Rolodex and other older organization methods with more efficient and effective ways of searching. Having the infrastructure in place to be able to mine a database provides opportunities that are not easily seen. For example, if I know that a good referral for you would be a financial adviser, I can rely on my memory or my notes—or an up-to-date database.

Embrace the mindset that today's technology needs to be an integral part of your networking activities. Technology enables you to scale, simplify, and speed processes up.

BUILD RELATIONSHIPS

Let's continue with the value of building relationships. There is an adage that says that "people do business with those they know, like, and trust" much more than they will with those they don't know, don't like, or don't trust.

Trust takes time, and it is earned. It takes multiple interactions before somebody trusts—and keep in mind that you can also eradicate trust with one bad interaction. So having the mindset of looking for ways

to build trust to prove yourself in the minds of others will help you make wise decisions.

Find ways to learn about and help others. This shows that you are not only good at what you do, but also

(1) are knowledgeable

(2) provide good products or services

(3) are a trustworthy person

(4) will do what you say you will do, and

(5) are reliable.

Trust takes time, and it is earned. Your word means something.

FACE-TO-FACE NETWORKING

Face-to-face (F2F) networking is key to your overall sales and referral success. When you decide to attend a live networking event or join a networking group, keep the mindset of being of value to those with whom you are interacting.

A big reason why I go to networking events is to find other resources I can bring to my referral partners and to my clients. And as a result, people really want to network with me because they know that I'm looking out for them…and of course, once I'm looking out for other people, the odds that they will look out for me increases significantly.

Face-to-Face Networking Opportunities

Vistage

ProVisors

YPO - Young Presidents' Organization

BNI - Business Network International

LeTip International

6 Degrees Business Networking

Chambers of Commerce

Convention and Visitor's Bureau

Small Business Development Center

Local Merchant Association

Trade Association

Meetup Group

Rotary

Kiwanis

Optimists

Soroptimists

Sometimes you can earn a person's predisposition to trust you by social proof.

When there are enough other people who are vouching for you, you gain trust. You didn't earn it directly with that person, but somebody is transferring it to you. So, put yourself in a position where some of the trust that is required for people to refer business to you is also earned through others.

Summary

You need the right mindset and infrastructure to become an effective networker.

Furthermore, you need the ability to execute. This way of thinking is as applicable in sports as it is in business. When you have a sports goal, you must prepare and practice. Nutrition, flexibility, connections, opportunities, and resiliency are vital components in reaching your goals. It's about committing to a game plan and saying, "We've practiced this. We've committed to this. And we believe that if we stay on track and we execute, we are going be in the best position to succeed."

If you want to be world-class in achieving your goals—whether in sports or in business—you need a plan that encompasses the entire picture. That's the goal of *The Referral Playbook: How to Increase Sales with Proven Networking Strategies*.

QUALITY EQUIPMENT TO WIN

We now have the mindset of being of value to people as a technology-empowered connector. To keep our connections alive, we need interactions and conversations.

Be Ready to Take the Time

If you're going to be farming and not hunting, many of the referrals and/or the sales that will take place will happen over time—sometimes three, six, nine months or longer. I've had people contact me to join my Vistage group after a year of staying in touch with them.

This process takes time because you are building relationships. People need to know, like, and trust you—*and* the timing needs to be right for them.

This progression happens over time and after several interactions. Your job is to stay involved with your contacts, ensuring you remain visible. It's hard to forge relationships when you are out of sight—and therefore out of mind.

How do you best organize this process of staying in touch and visible?

Invest in the right equipment.

The first step to having a good sporting experience is to buy equipment that is right for you—not necessarily the "best" or the most expensive. For instance, a professional tennis player may need a racquet that delivers a 130 mph serve, whereas you may play a better game with one that provides an 80 mph serve.

When choosing your **technology tools**, there's no "one size fits all." There are many options in the marketplace. I will share with you the software products I use, and I'll explain why I chose them. I'll also provide you with alternatives, in case the products I use seem too high-powered or high-priced for your needs.

DATABASE EQUIPMENT

As you might surmise, it can be difficult to keep up with all the people with whom you want to build relationships. The answer to this quandary is to use a database or client relationship management (CRM) program.

Today's technology tools put the process together. Let me be perfectly clear: technically, they give you the capability of putting together a process, but just because you have the capability doesn't mean that's all there is to do.

The phrase "use it or lose it" fits the bill here. Every contact you neglect to enter into your database is business lost. If you commit to using your system, it allows you to manage multiple contacts and to scale your referral gathering activities versus having to keep it all in your head, on Post-It Notes, or in a Rolodex. Use technology to facilitate the process of staying in touch.

Systems give you the power to close deals like never before by increasing productivity, keeping your pipeline filled with solid leads and scoring more wins.

Tools like Salesforce, Infusionsoft®, ZOHO, Microsoft Outlook, and more help you build relationships one interaction at a time. Just remember, those interactions must be mutually beneficial ones. If you call somebody and you say, "Hey, do you have referrals?" And a week later call and ask them, "Met any new people who could use my service?" You'll quickly become a nuisance and very few people will give you referrals.

However, if you put yourself in their shoes, engage with them on something that's important to them (as most people are more interested in themselves than in anyone else), you will add value to your relationship.

Salesforce

I use Salesforce because it is an excellent tool, and it is required by Vistage, the company in which I hold a position of Vistage Chair.

Salesforce is a high-end tech tool to manage contacts and track opportunities from any desktop or device. It integrates clean and enhanced B2B customer data with sophisticated data solutions to improve sales and marketing.

An alternative solution might be to use the contact address book in Microsoft Outlook that is included with your software bundle (and therefore has no additional cost).

Cost: $1000+ per year based on the number of users you have.

For more information or to sign up go to:
https://www.salesforce.com/

Infusionsoft®

I also use Infusionsoft because it allows me to preprogram content, segment it according to various criteria, and automate the process to control the frequency with which I deliver content to my target markets. Because I sell online products, I need a system that can manage my sales messages, autoresponders, product delivery, and the e-commerce end of the sales. Infusionsoft provides a tremendous opportunity to automate these things.

Cost: $99 per month package for managing 500 contacts and delivering 2,500 emails per month, plus other options.

Check it out at https://www.infusionsoft.com/

ZOHO

This cloud-based database service helps you manage contacts, activities, and, most importantly, your time, by keeping your notes, history, and interactions together in one organized place. You can also easily send and track professional email campaigns. Keeping contact information organized is crucial to your bottom line. When your information is spread across multiple platforms and products, you lose both time and a complete view of your customers' needs. ZOHO collects all your customer data in one place, surfacing the right information at the right time so you can present the right message.

Cost: $180-$280 per year (based on a variety of plans)

Check it out at https://www.zoho.com/

Remember…

If I would like referrals from you, the odds of your providing me with introductions are higher if I give you value.

Why?

Because as human beings, we are social people who want to reciprocate. And all things being equal, if somebody helps us out, we're likely to want to help them over someone who hasn't.

REFERRAL BUILDING EQUIPMENT

LinkedIn®

LinkedIn is a tool to support your trust-building. It allows you to become a connector. LinkedIn is used as a first point of contact that gives you visibility and reach.

For my line of work, when I meet somebody offline, my first action is to send him or her a LinkedIn invitation.

Rather than take their business card and enter all their details into another customer relationship management tool, I use LinkedIn to gather some basic information. I then start conversations using an invitation and LinkedIn's messenger.

Once we are connected, LinkedIn allows me to be visible to that person's connections and also allows me to search for particular professions connected to my new contact. Essentially, LinkedIn is a giant database that allows you to find more targeted people. If you use LinkedIn effectively, it will give you the opportunity to identify mutual connections.

Again, it's not just about having a profile on LinkedIn—it's how you use it as well. Keep your profile complete and up-to-date, as it acts as your mini sales page.

If you do an impressive job of creating a thorough profile, it helps your new connections feel like they know you better, and they will start to believe that you know what you're talking about in your industry.

If you don't have a LinkedIn account, start one today! But please remember, a poor LinkedIn profile is worse than none.

LinkedIn recommendations add trust

LinkedIn's feature of being able to ask for and give people recommendations adds trust. A recommendation on LinkedIn is different from recommendations garnered in many other places because it can be traced back directly to the individual.

If you receive a testimonial, somebody can click on it and know that you exist. They can read your profile, which gives them confidence that this was a real recommendation, a bona fide testimonial as opposed to one that was made up or paid for. In addition, you cannot change a single word of a recommendation or testimonial, which adds even more validity.

Cost: LinkedIn has a free basic plan. I use the Premium Plan, which offers more search filters at $49 per month.

To sign up go to: **https://www.linkedin.com**

BONUS OFFER: Email me at rick@rickitzkowich.com for a free copy of my "Monetize LinkedIn on 10 Minutes a Day Guide!"

Link Power Now

LinkedIn is the business professionals' social media platform. At first glance, it can be overwhelming. How do I put up my profile photo? What copy should I include in my summary or about my previous experience? And that's just the set-up piece of the puzzle!

I developed my Link Power Now (LPN) product to serve as a "how to" for maximizing a person's use of LinkedIn. Your LinkedIn page should be far more than an online parking spot for your resume.

So, if you haven't a clue why LinkedIn would be good for your business, Link Power Now will help you triple the number of referrals you give and receive, increase your revenue through referral marketing, and add to your word-of-mouth strategies.

Link Power Now consists of monthly "how to" videos with action steps to take for success. In addition, I make myself available for questions via phone, Skype, and email.

Cost: Link Power Now is $39 per month.

To purchase, go to:
http://ntwrk.biz/linkpowercoaching

Refer.com

Refer.com is another powerful platform. Refer.com gives you a platform to manage, build, and track your referral relationships. In a sense, it's another stay-in-touch technology tool, such as Infusionsoft or Salesforce, but it is more specifically geared toward the referral process.

Refer.com offers ways to stay relevant and to maintain contact so you can build relationships. "Mass personalization" is a term I use here. Though it sounds like an oxymoron, it's not. Let's say you have ten people who like drinking wine, and you have an article on wine. You can send that article as if it only went to one person.

With Refer.com, everything your prospects need to know about you is in one place. It's easy for others to refer you when they click on the **Refer Me** button on your Refer.com profile and also with your **Referral Card Email Signature**, which creates the opportunity for a quick connection. Your contact details are front and center, so people can quickly get ahold of you. Refer.com supports your brand and your story. A compelling headline entices your prospects to want learn more.

Say it, then back it up. With Refer.com, you can highlight your services, testimonials, referral team, and who's referred you in the past to put your best foot forward.

Cost: Refer.com has a free basic plan, yet I choose to use the $400 annual plan because it has the smart AI interface component, which allows me to send relevant content to my connections.

To sign up go to:
https://www.refer.com

Over the last few years, I have had the opportunity to personally meet with Tom Gay, CEO of Refer.com. During our lunches, we always seem to get into a lively exchange when we discuss the power of referrals. I thought it quite fitting to ask him to give his perspective on the importance of having a process in place for success.

Abundant Referrals in Just 10 Minutes a Day!

Most people know the "holy grail" of sales leads are referrals. They fully understand a well thought through referral generating strategy and plan is the best way to get more. Yet, the secret is that even with this knowledge so very few people actually do the things to ensure they gain that steady stream of new referred opportunities. Therein lies a huge opportunity for you as a reader of this book. I'll guarantee that when you decide to separate yourself from the majority and focus on building what I call a *systematic and repeatable* process to be more referable, you'll stand out. You win. You'll reach your sales goals!

I describe this systematic, repeatable process as a "10 minutes a day" focused keep-in-touch effort aimed at building strong, personal and trusted relationships with the people who are already doing business with your ideal target client. Think of it as taking the time you take every day to drink a cup of coffee and focus it on a few key people.

When you invest this small amount of energy on say 20-25 key people, in just a few short weeks, you'll gain six, eight, even 10 new closable sales leads each month. I've seen one professional consistently gain 15 referred leads a month by making a 10 minute a day concerted effort to build relationship bridges, gaining the resultant trust that comes with it. His key people are happy to open their iPhone / Rolodex contact list to let him scan and select who he'd like to meet.

Why does this work?

Well, when you invest in a person by making what you bring all about them and their interests, they very quickly want to reciprocate and give something of value back to you. It's just a natural honest human response.

Why don't more people do it?

My guess is that most people are just overwhelmed by all the noise in their lives, and they're unfocused. They don't know how to manage their time nor focus their efforts. They fail to build the proven habits that open the doors to big success. Yet, when one does, they become visible and stand out from the crowd and all the noise. More people want to know and work with them. Think of the word "scarcity." Why is gold so valuable? Because it's scarce! Think of the people you'd like to know and why. I'd bet there's something unique and scarce about them too. There's gold in those relationships!

**Tom Gay
CEO Refer.com**

I know this works as I used this focused process before starting Refer.com to build a new consulting practice. I gained 31 clients in just 18 months. You can do it too! You're on the right pathway here by investing in *The Referral Playbook*. It's filled with gold if you decide to focus on building your own "10 minutes a day" referral system. Decide now and get started today!

Rock-IT! Referrals

Rock-IT! Referrals (RIR) is a proven system to skyrocket referrals.

LinkedIn's powerful database combined with technology tools for screen sharing, content shortcuts, and online calendar scheduling creates a cost-effective, time-saving way to quadruple the number of targeted referrals you get from the people you know. Rock-IT Referrals includes video tutorials, "how to" eBooks, and template guides.

When I was faced with the challenge of building a group of local CEOs, I didn't want to do cold calling. I thought, what can I do to use my LinkedIn connections and my networking experience to facilitate the process? I first put out a request to my networking group that said, "I need introductions to CEOs of companies between $1M and $10M in annual revenue."

I got zero referrals from that strategy. I figured there was a disconnect there—because I knew those people wanted to help me. Rather than getting discouraged, **a light bulb came on—I had not made it easy for them to give me a referral.**

I proceeded to create a process we could do together to guide them through identifying who of their connections might be a fit for me. On my first day using it, I generated twenty-four referrals. After two weeks, I had received ninety-one introductions to local CEOs, fifty of whom I connected with on LinkedIn—this led to seventeen appointments—which converts to 19 percent results from the initial introductions.

Cost: $497

For more information or to purchase, go to:
http://ntwrk.biz/rockitreferrals

Referral Networking Face-to-Face

Local Business - Global Network®

BNI is an American franchised networking organization with around 200,000 members in 7,500 local chapters worldwide. Members meet regularly to discuss business and support each other's businesses by sharing referrals. I am especially partial to BNI because I was a member for more than seventeen years—serving as president of my BNI Del Mar chapter in San Diego for three terms. I have grown my business and established lifetime personal and professional relationships, and I attribute my overall networking success to BNI.

Founded in 1985 by Dr. Ivan Misner in Arcadia, California, BNI has earned recognition as being the world's greatest business referral organization. BNI has grown to include over 230,000 members worldwide, with chapters in over 70 countries across the globe. In 2017 alone, millions of BNI referrals led to $13 billion in sales worldwide.

The best way to find out more about how BNI works is to go to a local chapter meeting and see for yourself what it's like. After you've visited and decided that BNI is worth the investment, it's time to make a commitment, join the local chapter, and start giving and getting referrals—you'll develop long-lasting relationships that are more than just swapping business cards. The BNI slogan "Givers Gain" is what it's all about. This philosophy is key to the mindset you need to succeed.

By joining BNI, through its weekly meetings and exclusive resources, you'll increase your exposure to like-minded professionals, gain referrals from a global network, and sharpen your business networking skills with exclusive resources.

Cost: BNI annual dues are $500-$600. Individual chapters have a monthly fee based on the meeting room and food served, estimated at $64-$88 per month.

To learn more about BNI go to: https://www.bni.com

To find a BNI chapter near you, go to: https://www.bni.com/find-a-chapter

RELATIONSHIP BUILDING EQUIPMENT

Mackay 66 Spreadsheet

This tool was designed by Harvey Mackay of the well-known business books *How To Swim With The Sharks Without Being Eaten Alive* and *Beware The Naked Man Who Offers You His Shirt*. The Mackay 66 Spreadsheet is a time-honored, tried and proven tool that will help you build your business.

Mackay created and used the spreadsheet when he was running his successful envelope company. His goal was to create a list template to help him know his customers better than they knew themselves. He then used this knowledge to build rapport, make the sale, and surprise them with great service.

It includes such questions as "favorite places for lunch," "conversation interests," and "social organizations."

The 66 questions give you the edge on your competition when it comes to knowing your customers.

After I find out what your interests are, I can connect to you in a personal way. Let's say I find out that you're into craft beers, so on your birthday, I give you a gift related to the craft beer scene. Or if you're into sports or a fan of a team and I let you know when I come across an article or perhaps some tickets, that lets you know that I care about you as an individual.

The 66 questions are a strategic step to finding out specific information about your referral sources that will help you be of more value to them and help you build a relationship.

Purchase Harvey Mackay's book *Swim With the Sharks Without Being Eaten Alive* to find his highly regarded 66-Question Customer Profile.

Go to: http://www.harveymackay.com/books/

STAY-IN-TOUCH EQUIPMENT

QuoteActions

https://www.getquoteactions.com

One of the problems that I see when it comes to stay-in-touch technology tools start at the beginning, when individuals send and/or receive invitations to connect. On LinkedIn, for example, they treat the interaction like a monologue. They establish the connection and that's the end of it.

Instead, I see interactions on LinkedIn and other forums as opportunities to have conversations. So this is what I do: I send you an invitation to connect, and you accept it. The very next thing I do is send a thank you message for being connected to me, as well as to offer you something.

Now, this offering is a small token that says, "You know what? I value you." It's a custom in many cultures that, if you go to someone's home, you bring them a little gift. You give them a bottle of wine, you bring cookies, flowers—something to say "Thank you for your hospitality."

Well, take that concept and expand it. I've been using this method for years, and what I've learned is that, if you give something related to your business to someone when you first meet them, it's going to be received as marketing.

If you give something that is unrelated to what you do for business, yet related to the person, then it feels more personal. One way to employ this method is by using my QuoteActions.

Contact's First Name Appears →

Prewritten Content →

QuoteAction

Dear Sue,

> Here's your "QuoteAction" of the day:
>
> *"If you don't like something change it. If you can't change it, change your attitude."*
> **Best Selling Author, Maya Angelou**
>
> *Your action for today is to look at something in your life that you have failed to change. See if changing your attitude makes a difference.*
>
> Have an extraordinary day!

Your Contact Information — You decide what info you want to include! →

Ric LeVander 760-632-9390
CalDRE# 01460904
Christie Kramer-LeVander 760-632-9302
CalDRE# 00902753
Sea Coast Exclusive Properties
www.coastalhomespecialist.com

in Share Like Tweet

People can share your QuoteActions via social media. →

– To unsubscribe, change frequency or email Press here
– If you received this as a forward and want to subscribe to QuoteActions – Press here
– Send QuoteActions to your contacts, prospects, family and friends Press here

People can easily unsubscribe. →

If people receive the QA as a FWD, they can easily subscribe. →

Christie Kramer-LeVander
2146 Encinitas Blvd. Suite 110
Encinitas, CA 92024

Your Address Info ←

Sea Coast
EXCLUSIVE PROPERTIES

Your Photo ↑   **Your Logo** ↑

I created **QuoteActions** in 2007 to solve the problem of staying in front of my clients. Since then, thousands of individuals have received positive messages in their inbox.

The senders of the QuoteActions have meanwhile reaped the financial benefits of staying top-of-mind with their contacts—when they were ready to buy, they called them!

Here is the template to use with QuoteActions as a follow-up message after you connect with someone on LinkedIn. Or you can adapt the verbiage to work for connecting with someone after meeting them at a networking event.

Dear Name,

Now that we are connected here on LinkedIn, I look forward to getting to know you better and seeing how we might be able to help each other out.

I'm a firm believer that you must first give to receive. This "givers gain" approach has proven to be very effective for me in my face-to-face networking. Because I would like to continue to build our relationship, I'd like to offer you a gift—something I hope will be an uplifting, useful, and thought-provoking moment in your day.

My gift is an invitation to receive QuoteActions. They are short email messages containing a witty, interesting, and/or inspirational quote followed by a recommended action to help positively impact your day. I've found that QuoteActions give me a terrific start to my day—and something to think about!

Here's an example…

"Talent without discipline is like an octopus on roller skates. There's plenty of movement, but you never know if it's going to be forward, backwards, or sideways." – H. Jackson Brown, Jr.

Your action for today is to finish a project you have been procrastinating.

I hope you enjoy QuoteActions. There's no charge. It is simply a way I can give back to those who are making the world a better place in some way. You can choose how often you receive them and can unsubscribe at any time.

Please use this link if you would like to accept this gift:

http://www.quoteactions.com/a/profile/XXX

(Insert YOUR QuoteActions link)

Contact me with any questions you may have about QuoteActions.

Warmest Regards,
(Insert YOUR contact information)

QuoteActions are an appropriate gift or token for someone you've just met. It's a simple way to give them something. Plus, when someone accepts the QuoteActions invitation, it's like getting a magazine subscription. Every time the magazine shows up, the person thinks fondly of you, because you gave them something that was of value.

Cost: $1 the first month, then $34.95/month or $359/yr.

If you are interested in using QuoteActions as your gift or to just stay top-of-mind with your contacts and prospects, learn more and purchase at: https://www.getquoteactions.com

Birthday Alarm

Another tool I use to send digital birthday cards and gifts is **Birthday Alarm**. I have found that most people like to be recognized on their birthdays. While a physical card is even better, sending an animated digital card is the next best thing. Birthday Alarm keeps track of and reminds you about birthdays.

While you can have reminders with your other database management tools, Birthday Alarm helps me easily recognize people on their actual birthday.

Cost: Basic reminder service is free.

Sign up at: https://www.birthdayalarm.com

Send Out Cards

Send Out Cards is an online service that allows you to easily send physical cards and gifts from anywhere. Their wide selection of cards can be used to do more than simply recognize birthdays or holidays. They can be simple hellos or high-fives, thank you for your business, or an "I was thinking about how this might help you" message.

Send Out Cards' gift option is a nice bonus extra. You can easily ship six delicious brownies to someone—thanking them for the sweet deal they got you because of a referral to their car salesman. Or send a basket of lotions to someone who is recovering from surgery.

Cost: Basic plan $39 per month—with postage and gift selections extra.

Sign up at: https://www.sendoutcards.com

PRODUCTIVITY EQUIPMENT

TimeTrade

One of the biggest challenges I have is trying to book appointments. Trying to get somebody on the phone, especially the first time, is hard.

With a productivity tool like **TimeTrade**, you have a link where individuals can set appointments with you. For example, I have a link to my calendar where I make myself available between certain hours—let's say daily between 1 p.m. and 5 p.m. During those hours, people can book appointments with me. I simply set a link for an amount of time, say 15 or 30 minutes. People click on that link. They see my calendar in their own time zone and can immediately book an appointment with me at a time that's mutually convenient without us having to go back and forth.

TimeTrade provides a better customer experience. The integrated online appointment scheduling can help you deliver the responsiveness prospects and customers crave.

It also helps you stand apart from your competition by offering a "we've been expecting you" service guarantee that turns prospects into customers and your customers into brand ambassadors, all while increasing customer lifetime value.

Cost: $49 per year

Sign up at: https://www.timetrade.com

SANEBOX

Answering emails is easily one of the most time-consuming tasks of the work day. Current research data suggests, on average, business professionals can spend more than 3 hours reading, writing and sending emails daily. That equates to more than 15 hours a week. Even on vacation, people fall victim to sorting through junk email.

SaneBox is the single best product I've found for reducing email noise. I had tried other services to no avail. It's truly incredible. I literally was inundated with junk email. I found the time I spent sorting and deleting emails was cutting deeply into my productivity.

SaneBox moves unimportant emails out of your Inbox and summarizes them in a digest. This feature alone saves time and helps you focus on emails that matter to you. You can even snooze important but non-urgent emails until they are actionable. And, you'll never forget to follow up on opportunities with automatic follow up reminders.

With SaneBox you'll be proactive, not reactive. It's integrated with Salesforce and works anywhere you check your email with an easy slope learning curve.

Cost: Packages start at $7 per month for one email address.

Sign up at: https://www.sanebox.com

ACTIVEWORDS

ActiveWords is an efficiency tool that allows me to program copy with keyboard shortcuts. Let's say I want to program the word "password" or even multiple passwords. If I program the letters PW, then click a key on my computer, it will type in the password for a particular website so I don't have to remember it.

Or I can also write emails using ActiveWords if there are certain responses that I give consistently. It saves a tremendous amount of time compared to copying and pasting. Additionally, it can open programs for you, saving time, improving accuracy, and helping you get results.

With all your technology, not just ActiveWords, simplify your messages. Think ahead on how you can incorporate personalization.

Rather than having to type a unique response every single time, write it in a way that allows you to use your message again and again. Or prepare a video that can go to multiple people or be used to answer a question you often receive. Not only does your technology help your efficiency, but your initial setup allows you to maximize mass personalization.

ActiveWords saves tons of time typing the same messages; it's even more efficient than using copy-paste methods.

Cost: $30 per year

Sign up at: https://www.activewords.com/

UASSIST.ME - VIRTUAL ASSISTANT

Sometimes I'm told, "You know, Rick, I just don't have the time to do all the action items you suggest. Whether it's sending out email invitations to receive my QuoteActions or entering contacts I meet at networking events into a database, I am already too busy." My answer to them is: you can't afford not to make time **OR** identify a solution. Because without follow-up and stay-in-touch strategies in place, you're fishing for referrals with a pole, not a net.

You'll never be able to get ahead without systems in place. We're lucky to have technology on our side! The internet allows you to hire a **Virtual Assistant (VA)** to help with administrative, creative, and technical services. Did you know you can save 77% on what you would spend on an in-house or staff person? It pays to look into outsourcing non-core activities so you can focus on what you really need to be doing.

I have had a VA through a company called UAssist.Me for more than six months now. It's great. I work with the same person, and she understands my style of work. I may need research done for an article, my handwritten notes digitized, new contacts entered into my database, social media posts, and more.

UAssist.Me is based in Miami Beach, Florida, and offers their virtual personal and business assistant services in English and in Spanish. The VAs help you grow your business by eliminating the need to spend valuable time on administrative tasks that do not require strategic decision-making.

The process is easy. Choose one of the plans, interview and meet your new assistant, and begin delegating. The high-touch onboarding process has been carefully crafted, ensuring that you get all the information and training you need to start effectively delegating and using your new assistant immediately.

Cost: $15-$35 per hour—through different plans, based on types of services and hours per month.

To learn more or use the service, go to: https://www.uassistme.co/

GAME STRATEGIES

With the right mindset and tech equipment in hand, here are some tactics that can take your networking success to a higher playing field.

CONVERSATIONS VS. MONOLOGUES

While we touched on this concept in the section on LinkedIn, it's important to understand that as human beings we crave relationships, especially in this day and age when there are so many ways to be pseudo-engaged with people through likes, connections, and followers.

If you watch, you'll see that during the networking process, most interactions are a solicitation to buy/sell products or to check out something for someone else's business.

The fact of the matter is that people pay attention and/or notice when someone goes out of their way to be human. One way to do this is through conversations.

My goal as I interact with others is to be a conversation starter.

I try to engage with many, many people, yet I can only have conversations with people who respond to me. These are the people who perhaps will lead to something or perhaps not. Regardless, I lay the foundation for a later interaction. Whatever direction the engagement takes, I consistently have people who are impressed with the humanness of how I reach out.

I also use the tech tools we discussed in the previous chapter to capture and remember details about individuals, which helps the people I interact with feel important.

These tools sweeten your tactics. They not only facilitate greater depth between yourself and others, but also enable you to view your contacts through the lens of many of their skills, interests, and businesses.

With only a business card in hand, we tend to see others as one-dimensional because it tells us so little about them.

However, as we have further conversations and use our stay-in-touch tools, we learn about and ultimately care about them even more.

MAKE DEPOSITS BEFORE WITHDRAWALS

If we think about relationships like a checking account, to write checks and make sure they don't bounce, we first need to make deposits.

If you are making a deposit in a relationship by giving something valuable to the person, and you do that consistently over time, the odds are greater that, when you do ask for something in return, it will be likely to happen.

I recommend seeking ways to make deposits of resources, information, and introductions to create goodwill in the minds of the people with whom you are connected.

It's all about you going first…

You going first in the giving.

You going first in offering value.

You extending yourself. It's even as simple as smiling first.

Stay Top-of-Mind

Staying top-of-mind means finding a way for people to think of you more frequently. Odds are that people would refer to you more often if they only thought about you at the time when the opportunity occurred.

Of course, advertising is designed to do that—to remind people that the product or the service exists. People remember an ad when a need or an urge arises. Let's say you are hungry. And right then, you see an advertisement for pizza. You're much more likely to order pizza when the need, in this case hunger, is presenting itself.

It's the same thing with our products and services. If you find a way to remind people that you exist and you're seeking business, they will be thinking of you when the right opportunity comes up for them to refer you.

Do not assume that because people have known you for a long time, they will automatically refer to you.

Add Value to Your Interactions

One major concern we all have is the line between bothering people and staying in touch.

People are worried about how much is too much—and we all have assumptions as to where this line occurs. But the reality is, we don't know.

As I'm writing this, I'm experiencing this myself. Just yesterday, there was a contact that I've been checking in with periodically regarding one of my services.

And she responded to me saying, "One of the things I really admire about you is your persistence and the way that you follow up." We now have an appointment tomorrow because I've been able to follow up, and I've been able to stay top-of-mind with this person.

Certainly, people react differently, but I do know that the more options you have available, the more your name will be used and shared.

The trick is to stay as relevant as possible, and that requires either some information or some communication to find out what is or isn't applicable to that individual.

The key in terms of frequency is that you are still giving something that is relevant to them and that they perceive that you're trying.

Sending someone a useful article, infographic, or referral doesn't require much effort. Moreover, it shows you care enough to give one of your most valuable resources, which is time, to try to provide something that you know is relevant.

Track Referrals: The 80/20 Rule

The **Pareto Principle** says that you should invest 80 percent of your activities with the top 20 percent of your people. So, the majority of what you do should follow the 80-20 rule. In order to determine who the best or the most profitable contacts are, you need to track this information. For instance, if I have two people, and one of them is reciprocating more than the other, I will continue to give more to the person who reciprocates. This is a simple concept. However, it is too hard to remember all of this on your own.

Find a tracking system that works for you to be able to identify your contact sphere and who your main reciprocators are.

ESTABLISH METRICS

When I talk about establishing metrics, I mean establishing metrics based on activities for which you have 100 percent control over what you do on your end, rather than on how the person responds.

In the sales process, for instance, I tell people to consider the notion of a phone call. You dialing is entirely up to you. But whether or not someone answers is out of your control. The connection is not entirely up to you, though you can initiate the potential for connection. Let's relate that to metrics.

Numbers can be your friends regarding your ability to project and to scale your business. That you need to talk to somebody, say, twenty-five times before they'll agree to something is an important metric to know. When you are putting together plans for scaling, you need to know if five referral sources get one referral. If so, then to get five referrals, you will need twenty-five referral sources.

Numbers are important if you want to become more strategic in your networking with the ability to scale because you can then work with more predictability.

REVERSE ENGINEER GOALS

Reverse engineer goals and connect them to activities. What does this mean?

If you know that your average sale is, let's say, $10, and you want to get $100 in sales, then you're going to need ten sales to achieve that goal. To get one sale, you need to talk to ten different people. Hence, you're going to need to talk to one hundred different people to get ten sales.

What happens in the reverse engineering process is that you start with the result and work backwards to see what activities you need to do. Again, this is where tracking helps. If you want to be more in control of getting the referrals, you need to practice reverse engineering.

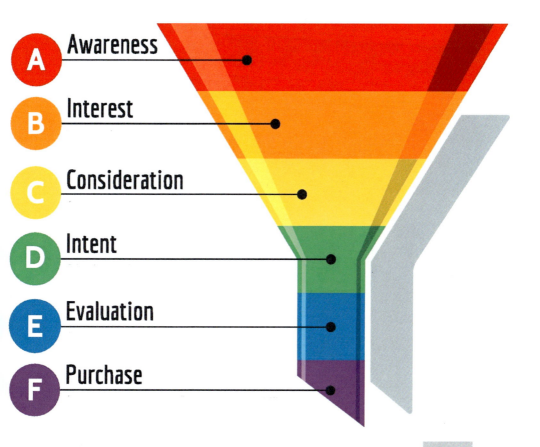

You need to determine, on average, if you need to reach out five or seven or more times before you will be able to ask for and receive referrals or make a sale.

Remember: Start out with the desired result, and then work backwards to determine the different points that will lead you to achieving your objective.

GATHER INTELLIGENCE

The Mackay 66 is a tool we discussed in the "Quality Equipment" section. Harvey Mackay sought to find out all kinds of information about his customers. This ranged from interests in their family, schools, hobbies, and more—this knowledge put him in a position to give targeted and relevant gifts. He could also provide information and advice that would resonate with his contacts.

When you are assessing your customers, a key point is to also understand how age plays a role in using your tools in a tactical manner. Facebook, LinkedIn, Twitter, Instagram, and Pinterest each have general age ranges. Be sure you are aware of your contact's age range so you can choose the appropriate platform. It will also help you find relevant pieces that can strengthen your relationship and show that you are indeed going out of your way to establish a reciprocal connection based on the person's technological style and language.

In the same way that giving a custom gift is more meaningful than a generic one, this attention to detail is more personal and makes it easier for them to refer to you, and you to them.

It all boils down to finding and providing relevant information and pathways to reach your prospects and stay top-of-mind with your top customers and referral sources.

FOUR KEY GAME COMPONENTS

To play the game of sales and referrals through both online and offline networking/engagement strategies, we need to introduce the four key components: Goals, People, Content, and Process.

If your average sale is **$1,000**, and your **goal is $10,000 in sales**—you're going to need **10 sales** to achieve that goal. To get **one sale**, you need to **talk to ten** different people. So, you'll need to **talk to one hundred** different people **to get ten sales**.

At first, you will guesstimate your leads goal, and then adjust it as you track your data in your database software.

Face-to-Face (FTF) Networking
Structured / Misc. 1x Events
Online Networking
LinkedIn / Refer.com
Trusted Advisors
Connections Who Can Help Your Contacts
Social Events
Clubs / Sports / Hobbies Groups
Existing Connections / Customers
Referral Sources
i.e. CPAs, Financial Planners

CONTENT	PROCESS
Daily / Weekly QuoteActions Personalized Automated Messages	**Developing Your Sales Funnel by Efficiently Engaging People Through...**
Monthly Relevant Articles Using Refer.com AI Service	**Online Networking** LinkedIn / Refer.com
Birthday Wishes Birthday Alarm / Send Out Cards	**Offline Networking** BNI, Organizations and 1x Events
Information-based Reports Mail Chimp / Refer.com / Constant Contact	**Tools to Use** Rock-IT! Referrals McKay 66 Spreadsheet TimeTrade & ActiveWords
Events / Webinars / Podcasts Eventbrite / Email Blasts	

After you review the four key components, take the four-part assessment of the basic skill sets you need to play the game:

1. Mindset—Generosity
2. Database—Management
3. Offline Networking
4. Online Networking

MINDSET TO WIN

Do you have the mindset to succeed at networking to reap long-term profits?

A generosity mindset starts with a belief system. To find out if you have it, answer the questions below honestly with a YES or NO. Please do not give yourself a "YES" unless you have done the actions within the last month.

1. Have you had any interactions with people—customers or prospects—that were not directly related to business (a sales call to someone or a follow-up email on a business in progress does not count)?

2. Have you sent birthday greetings—either through a call, online, or a physical card—to at least two connections?

3. Do you have a system in place to record and track your connections' personal interests, e.g. football, fine wine, camping?

4. Have you forwarded an interesting information-based article to a person you would like to do business with?

5. Do you attend networking events for the sole purpose of finding referrals for your trusted advisors or referral team?

Give yourself 5 points for every YES.

25 pts.	You've got the mindset!
20 pts.	Just a few more tips will help you nail it!
15 pts.	Maybe signing up for Birthday Alarm will help.
10 pts.	Might want to make time for these activities.
5 pts.	It's okay, you've got this playbook for help.

EQUIPMENT TO WIN

Do you have a database in place to manage, track, and measure your success with your pipeline of people?

To find out if you have an adequate database system in place, answer the following questions honestly with a YES or NO.

1. Do you currently have and consistently use a database contact management system such as Salesforce, Infusion Soft, ZOHO, or Outlook?
2. Do you have custom fields for titles, birthdays, interests, industries, organizations, anniversaries, and how you met?
3. After networking events, do you send a LinkedIn invite to connect as well as enter all your new connections into your database?
4. Can you or someone on your team easily export your database into .csv format for upload to other stay-in-touch tools like Mail Chimp or Constant Contact?
5. Does your database have reminder features built in?

Give yourself 5 points for every YES.

25 pts.	You've got the equipment in place!
20 pts.	Just a few more how-to tips will help you nail it!
15 pts.	Consider a database system with more bells.
10 pts.	Might want to hire a Virtual Assistant to input data.
5 pts.	Must start somewhere—it's okay. Sign up for a database system.
0 pts.	Have your local computer support person help you out.

OFFLINE PLACES TO WIN

Do you have face-to-face networking organizations in place to meet people for your pipeline?

Trade/ Pro	Non-Profit	Networking	Community	Adult Family
USC Alumni	Rotary	ProVisors	Temple Beth El	Joe Smith
ELFA	Kiwanis	BNI	HOA	Andrea Bye
CalCPA	Soroptimist	Chamber	Tennis Team	Bob Noman

The chart above will help you identify the types of organizations you can use to create a constant flow of new "suspects" or "prospects" for your sales and referral farming. Without people, the system doesn't work.

To establish if you have enough sources to feed your funnel, answer the following questions with a YES or NO.

1. Are you involved in at least three offline face-to-face (F2F) organizations to feed your database on a regular basis?

2. Offline events/meetings should rank as high on your calendar as business appointments. Do you attend at least one event per month?

3. Many folks attend events and hang out with the same people. When you attend events, do you make it a point to focus on meeting new people?

Give yourself 5 points for every YES.

15 pts.   You have a strong offline foundation in place.

10 pts.   It won't take much to punch up your offline plan.

5 pts.   You may need to bump up your commitment.

0 pts.   Set a goal to join two organizations.

ONLINE PLACES TO WIN

Do you have a strong online presence?

1. Is your LinkedIn profile fully completed? This includes a customized URL, professional photo, 300-word summary, career experience, membership in organizations, volunteer experience, and education.

2. Do you have a repeatable strategy to use LinkedIn to generate introductions and leads? This includes setting aside time at least once a week to do LinkedIn searches for your customer matches, asking for introductions, and following up.

3. Have you signed up for Refer.com?
   You design and share your personal referral card, which includes your background and contact information through built-in emails, surveys, and social sharing tools.

4. Have you signed up for and are you using Refer.com's Engage program? This unique service helps you expand your network by deepening business relationships through sending regular SMART communications on topics your contacts are interested in.

Give yourself 5 points for every YES.

20 pts.	You are knocking it out of the park!
15 pts.	You are on your way to significantly magnifying your reach to fill your pipeline.
10 pts.	Check out whichever online platform you are not on, and join it today!
5 pts.	You've dipped your toes in the pool, now swim!
0 pts.	Time to ask for some help, you'll be glad you did.

PUTTING YOUR GAME PLAN TOGETHER

When you first start putting your game plan together, guesstimate the number of people you need to meet and interact with to make a sale based on your previous experience. Once you have the number of leads you need to generate, you must select both **Build Plays** and **Visibility Plays** to feed this pipeline. The winning formula is to become someone people know, like, and trust so that, when they are ready to buy, they immediately think of you and have your contact information handy.

GOAL SETTING

Start with the result you want to achieve and go backwards in order to select the plays that will yield the number of prospects you need each month in your pipeline.

EXAMPLE

If you know that your average sale is, let's say, $10, and you want to get $100 in sales, then you're going to need 10 sales to achieve that goal.

In order to get one sale, you need to talk to 10 different people. So, you're going to need to talk to 100 different people to get 10 sales.

BUILD PLAYS

Professional Organizations
Face-to-Face Networking (F2F)
One-to-One Meetings (121)

LinkedIn Search
Online Networking
Refer.com

Community / Clubs / Sports
Social Events

Existing Contacts
Rock-IT Referral Session (RIR)

Referral Sources
Rock-IT Referral Session (RIR)

VISIBILITY PLAYS

Salesforce (or Database)
Upload and Update
Keep Current

Refer.com
Send Targeted Articles
Email News

QuoteActions
Send Invitations

Birthday Alarm
Send Cards

Send Out Cards
Send Snail Cards or Gifts

Eventbrite
Create Events

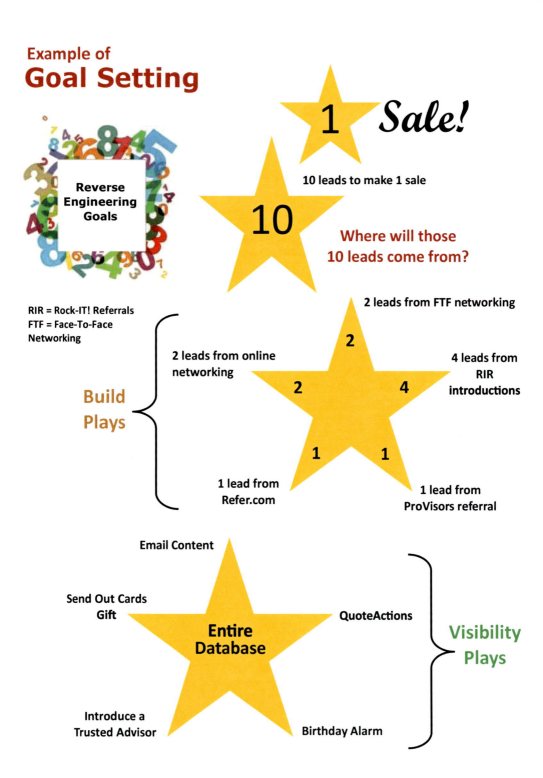

Example of
Goal Setting

1 ★ Vistage Member

Reverse Engineering Goals

```
Future Follow-up | Disqualified → Attend Mtg.   1 out of 3 move up
                   Disqualified → 75 min. Interview   1 out of 2 move up
                   Disqualified → 10 min. Qualify Call   1 out of 2 move up
                   Rock IT! Referral Session   1 out of 5 move up
                   FTF Networking              4 out of 5 move up
                   Referral Introduction
```

I know I need three people to attend an introduction meeting to get one new member for my group. Based on the chart, I need between fifteen and nineteen people on the front end of my pipeline to achieve this one new Vistage member for **my current group**.

In addition to generating members from prospects attending meetings, I've found that my visibility follow-up plays to people who attended meetings but didn't sign up has led to new members at a rate of 10 percent. So, if I continue to have one prospect attend one meeting per month, I'll be generating one additional sign up per year from my follow-up plays. What this does is reduce the number of prospects I need to generate every month.

Now, if I want to start **a new group**, I will need eight new sign ups—that's the minimum number to get a group launched. Using my statistics, I'll need enough plays to generate twenty-four attendees at a launch meeting. That equates to roughly 360-456 prospects. This is a much higher volume of required prospects than my current goal of having an existing group of eight CEOs. The plays that offer the best combination for generating a high volume of leads with a minimum investment of time are the Rock IT! Referral (RIR) plays. I can generate five leads per RIR play—although they will be lower quality leads, meaning I will book a ten-minute appointment with only 20 percent of them vs. 80 percent of the referral and F2F networking leads.

As you can see, the two plays are vastly different depending on my goals and the volume I need to generate.

BUILD PLAYS

Build Plays are designed to put you in front of a lot of people. The more people, the more opportunities you create. If you are not a seasoned networker, start out by using beginner plays. As you get the knack and become familiar with success, you'll want to add more activities to your game plays.

Over the next five pages, see three sample Build Plays.

Pipeline Build Play #1

Step 1: Using a spreadsheet format, set up your projected monthly goals. Until you have data to substantiate how many leads you'll get from different activities, simply guesstimate to get the ball rolling.

Step 2: By putting your activities, time, and budget in writing, you will see a direct correlation with the results. After the month is over, you can enter actual numbers in red to track them.

Name of Play	Category	Activity	Monthly Frequency	Monthly Budget $	Monthly Budget Time	Leads/Mo. Expected
ProVisors	F2F Networking	Attend Meeting	1	$150	2 hr	1
ProVisors	F2F Networking	121 Meeting	1	$20	2 hr	1
Industry Event	F2F Networking	Attend Event	1	$75	3 hr	1
LinkedInSearch	Online Networking	Search	4	$80	1 hr	4
Golf w Ref. Source	Social Event	Play 18 Holes	1	$160	6 hr	2
RIR Session	Existing Members	Screen Share	1	$0	1 hr	2
TOTALS			**9**	**$485**	**15 hrs**	**11**

BUILD PLAYS

The best part about using *The Referral Playbook* is that you have a process with tools in place and a measurable system that is scalable. You can ramp up or slow down your lead generation at any time based on the number and frequency of activities.

Pipeline Build Play #2

Step 1: Ideally, you will gain confidence in using new systems like Rock-IT Referrals (RIR) to generate introductions to your target prospects. When you get better and faster at it, you can schedule two—one with Referral Sources and one with Existing Members—to generate twice as many leads.

Step 2: Build Plays help you get over mindless networking syndrome. Having goals set for each event turns you into a networker with a purpose.

Name of Play	Category	Activity	Monthly Frequency	Monthly Budget $	Monthly Budget Time	Leads/Mo. Expected
BNI	F2F Networking	Attend Meeting	4	$70	12 hr	8
BNI	F2F Networking	121 Meeting	4	$80	8 hr	4
Chamber	F2F Networking	Event	1	$75	2 hr	3
LinkedIn Search	Online Networking	Search	8	$80	2 hr	8
RIR Session	Referral Sources	Screen Share	1	$0	1 hr	2
RIR Session	Existing Members	Screen Share	1	$0	1 hr	2
		TOTAL	**19**	**$305**	**26 hrs**	**27**

BUILD PLAYS

Tracking your results from Build Plays helps you identify your key organizations, your best networking style, and your favorite outside activities. Based on your results, you'll be able to input the frequency, budget, and time of what you are doing, along with accurate projections for meeting new people.

Pipeline Build Play #3

Step 1: Another bonus with this easy playbook system is that you'll soon find out where you are wasting your time. If, after three months of tracking leads from a certain type of alumni event, you come up empty-handed each time, you'll be able to make an educated decision to stop attending these types of events and put more time on your LinkedIn searches or referral source one-to-one (121) meetings.

Name of Play	Category	Activity	Monthly Frequency	Monthly Budget $	Monthly Budget Time	Leads/Mo. Expected
USC Alumni	F2F Networking	Attend Meeting	1	$80	2 hr	2
USC Alumni	F2F Networking	121 Meeting	2	$40	4 hr	4
Chamber	F2F Networking	Event	1	$35	2 hr	1
LinkedIn Search	Online Networking	Search	8	$80	2 hr	8
HOA Party	Social Event	Attend Event	1	$0	2 hr	1
RIR Session	Referral Sources	Screen Share	2	$0	2 hr	4
TOTAL			**15**	**$235**	**14 hrs**	**20**

86

VISIBILITY PLAYS

Visibility or Maintenance Plays are designed to help you stay involved with your contacts. You've used Build Plays to add prospects to your pipeline—now you need to consciously and systematically stay in front of them. It's tough to nurture relationships when you are out of sight and out of mind!

Over the next five pages, see three sample Visibility Plays.

Pipeline Visibility Play #1

Step 1: Using a spreadsheet/table format, set up your projected monthly goals. Until you set up and start using your various content accounts such as Refer.com, Birthday Alarm, QuoteActions, etc., guesstimate your budget numbers to get the ball rolling.

Step 2: A written plan helps you prioritize your stay-in-touch time and holds you accountable.

Name of Play	Category	Activity	Monthly Frequency	Monthly Budget $	Monthly Budget Time	Notes:
Salesforce	Database Mgmt.	Upload/Update	4	$99	1 hr	
Refer.com	Content	Send Articles	4	$50	1 hr	
QuoteActions	Content	Send Invites	8	$35	1 hr	
Birthday Alarm	Content	Send Cards	2	$5	1 hr	
Send Out Cards	Content	Send Gift	2	$40	1 hr	
Email Blast	Content	Information	2	$15	2 hr	
		TOTAL	**22**	**$244**	**7 hr**	

VISIBILITY PLAYS

The best part about using *The Referral Playbook* is that you now have a process in place that makes it easy to remember to reach out and interact with your pipeline. You never know whom they are talking to who might need your services, or if their situation has changed. They may be ready to buy when they receive your fourth monthly article.

Pipeline Visibility Play #2

Step 1: I often get asked, "Why so many content options? Are any more important than the others on the list?" The secret is in the number and variety of interactions, which allows you to create more "touches" without overdoing any one of them.

Step 2: Look for ways to make your life easier. Incorporate productivity tools like ActiveWords to streamline your content delivery.

Name of Play	Category	Activity	Monthly Frequency	Monthly Budget $	Monthly Budget Time	Notes:
ZOHO	Database Mgmt.	Upload/Update	8	$20	1 hr	
Refer.com	Content	Send Articles	4	$50	1 hr	
QuoteActions	Content	Send Invites	12	$35	1 hr	
BNI Connect	Content	BNI Member Introductions	4	$0	1 hr	
Send Out Cards	Content	Send Gift	4	$80	2 hr	
Podcast	Event	Send Invites	1	$0	3 hr	
TOTAL			**33**	**$185**	**9 hr**	

VISIBILITY PLAYS

Visibility Plays are ways to make deposits in your relationships by giving something that's considered valuable to the person. When you do this over time, the odds are that when you do ask for something in return—say, a referral—it's much more likely to happen. In addition, I strongly recommend introducing your prospects to trusted advisors.

Pipeline Visibility Play #3

Step 1: Of all the options for staying in touch, there's none easier than when someone accepts your QuoteActions invitation. It's like getting a magazine subscription. Every time the magazine shows up, the person thinks fondly of you because you gave them something of value. It's a tech tool you can use to offer something as a gift when you first meet someone or connect with them on LinkedIn. The only time you invest each month is in sending out invitations to receive QuoteActions. Once subscribed, they are delivered automatically!

Name of Play	Category	Activity	Monthly Frequency	Monthly Budget $	Monthly Budget Time	Notes:
Infusion Soft	Database Mgmt.	Upload/Update	8	$80	2 hr	
Refer.com	Content	Send Articles	4	$50	1 hr	
QuoteActions	Content	Send Invites	10	$35	1 hr	
Birthday Alarm	Content	Send Cards	4	$5	1 hr	
Mrs. Fields	Content	Send Cookies	2	$40	1 hr	
eBook	Content	Send eBook	1	$0	1 hr	
		TOTAL	**29**	**$210**	**7 hr**	

WHAT ABOUT?

As I neared the end of writing this book, I asked one of my trusted advisors to review the final proof. He asked me, "Rick, do you think you've answered all the questions people want answered when they finish reading your material? My answer was, "You know . . . I really can't be sure at this point."

For this reason, I used my networking circles. I reached out and asked my connections on LinkedIn and other sources to submit a question about online or offline networking. I included the selected questions and answers in the following five categories: mindset, connecting, personalities, network organization, and business management in networking.

MINDSET

Generations

Question:

The questions I have about networking are more "generational" at this point. When choosing professionals to work with, we know the old-school Silent Generation, Baby Boomers, and older Gen X all value "the handshake." They look someone in the eye, identifying their loyalty, and feel comfortable that they are conducting business with a person "of their word."

My question is how to establish these bonds with younger Gen X and Millennial generations. They appear to be more intent on doing business with "faceless professionals" online—circumventing seasoned professionals in the spirit of saving money, while pursuing their answers via Google rather than consulting directly with knowledgeable professionals.

How do we effectively achieve the same success with customers / affiliates / partners who are raised with different values—who prefer to avoid eye-contact and personal relationships with their sales / service professionals?

Please articulate how to successfully blend old school business development / retention methodology with new school best-practice methods.

Jason Gordon
Sr. Mortgage Loan Officer
Sr. Mortgage Loan Officer | NMLS 259027
AmeriFirst Financial, Inc. | NMLS 145368
www.GordonMortgage.com

Answer:

There's no question that networking with Gen X and Millennials, the people who grew up with technology, is going to be different from old school and baby boomers. While we all rely and depend more on technology than we ever did, the principles don't change, yet the approach does change.

First, it is essential to build your online credentials through one of the current methods—like LinkedIn and Refer.com. When you network with the younger generation, the latest tools will allow you to showcase your credibility and your expertise. In today's marketplace, people gauge how trustworthy you are based on an online component prior to talking to you. So, to answer your question, your online presence is going to be even more important than it's been in the past with people more accustomed to face-to-face networking.

The principles don't change. Truly the younger generation does value hard work, honesty, and credibility. How they arrive at that determination is influenced by the technology their lives have been inundated with over their lifetime. Thus, the importance of online tools plays a greater role with Gen X and Millennials *and* will continue to do so in the future.

Millennial Market

Question:

What do you believe is the best online marketing platform to use to reach the Millennial market? And how do you see it changing in the next few years? I know video is a large component, but do the platforms matter?

Edie Anne
Independent Scentsy SuperStar Director
Beauty n' Scents
www.BeautynScents.net

Answer:

The Millennial demographic attention span *is* best met with short videos. Quick, powerful clips will turn heads. I can't say for sure that they are only scanning one platform. I recommend you determine the platform(s) you choose as more strategy, as opposed to only one of your tactics.

How to identify the best online marketing platform is a tactical question. Tactics are pieces that you implement, but the strategy is the bigger picture. Develop a marketing strategy and build your tactics to ask questions in a way that will reach out to Millennials. Or better yet, make videos that specifically reach your target market.

I'm not sure Millennials can be categorized as your entire market. They may be a segment for you. Once you look at this segment from a marketing strategy perspective, as opposed to marketing tactic, you stand to have a more comprehensive approach, and as a result, you will be more successful.

Introductions

Question:

One thing I have found about offline networking is that other people appreciate proactive thinking about introductions. When you take time to assess who within your network the person you have just met would benefit meeting, you have discovered a big part of the power of networking. Do you have any suggestions on how people can be encouraged to think this way? I want to mention I only make an introduction when I'm comfortable there is a good match. I will spend time clarifying to find mutually beneficial links.

Robin Winnett
Managing Director
Kaizen Systems Limited
robin.w@kaizensystems.co.uk

Answer:

The more you operate this way with the people you meet, the more you educate them. You might bring this topic up in conversation. You can use it as a discussion point rather than coming across as telling them what to do. By sharing your experiences and examples, they will recognize the benefits of proactively finding introduction opportunities themselves.

When I go to a networking event, my primary reason for attending is to find people. I'm working to meet people, right in that moment, who I can introduce to people in my network or vice versa. I like being the introduction point person. People recognize that I can connect them to others, and that's useful to them. You and I are on the same page when it comes to this mindset. As others grasp this concept, they will see how helpful meaningful introductions can be now and in the future.

I encourage you to keep expanding this thought process. I always get a great response when I discuss this topic. Once you start sharing your goals with others, you'll be educating and bringing the mentality and mindset to your contacts and connections.

CONNECTING

Keeping In Touch

Question:

What is a recommended strategy for keeping in touch with your new prospects / referral sources without being an annoying pest?

Pete Tentler, CRMP
The Financial Locksmith®
Certified Reverse Mortgage Professional
https://www.linkedin.com/in/petetentler/

Answer:

Put yourself in the shoes of the person receiving the messages from you. My best recommendation is to send people information. Be creative and think of what they would like to receive. Avoid only focusing on what you want to send. You may have a generic article that might appeal to a lot of people in your field. Make sure it is something that is relevant and current. For example, "With the tax season coming up, here are the changes you can expect." Also, be sure you've read what you are sending out. Highlight some of the benefits that would be especially useful. The more you know about the people you're trying to communicate with, the more you can send them personal content that is of value to them.

Let's say you know someone who just had a baby; maybe send them some nonintrusive information on parenthood. If you are tactful and personal, your information will be welcome. This shows that you're thinking of them in a more personal way. There's a product called 'QuoteActions' that I developed exactly for this purpose. QuoteActions are inspirational, motivational quotes with an action connected to it—and you offer it to people as a gift.

Because QuoteActions is totally unrelated to your business, it's something you can give people, and they will not feel like you're trying to sell them anything. And, there's the added benefit that if someone accepts your invitation, they know they will be hearing from you on a regular basis without you being a pest. After all, they have accepted it and can unsubscribe at any time.

Referrals

Question:

What is the best way to ask someone for a referral *and* make the process as easy as possible to get the introduction you want?

Adam Harris
Director
Fresh Mindset UK Ltd
www.Fresh-Mindset.com

Answer:

First, a specific referral is better than a general referral. Therefore, if possible, narrow your "want" down to a specific company, as opposed to just an industry. If you have the person's name, that's even better. If you are making a request for referrals, you must make it easy for people to understand what you do–so they will think of you when they hear a need you fulfill. That's your networking job.

For example, there is one business attorney I know who specializes in partnerships. He's made it very easy for me to think of him when the right opportunity arises. Why is this important? Because I know many attorneys, but I rarely think of them off the top of my head—because the description of what they do is too general. This attorney has worked at positioning himself with me for a specific referral request. The easier you make it for people to refer you to someone, the more likely they are going to make the introduction.

Another referral best practice would be to use LinkedIn. It's a fabulous tool to easily get referrals. Let me share an example. When I was launching my Vistage group, I developed a process where, with permission, I logged into a referral source's LinkedIn account. This allowed us to search together the parameters I needed in order to reach the CEOs I wanted to meet. When we found good matches that they were connected to, I supplied a pre-written introduction message that my referral source could send to them. The process made it easy for individuals to edit the message and use it for other introductions in the future.

Remember, when asking someone for referrals be as specific as you can regarding the type of referral you want. Connect yourself with a need or situation. Once you've positioned yourself for the types of referrals you want, ensure the process is easy.

CEO Networking

Question:

My company is a member of the local chamber. Should I attend with my sales manager or is two a crowd for an evening mixer and not worth my time to attend?

Hashim Reza Taqvi
CEO
Taqvi Telecommunications
www.taqvitel.com

Answer:

The truth is when people go to networking events with someone they know, they end up spending more time with the people they know rather than mixing and mingling. Having a familiar face becomes a crutch, and it can hinder productivity.

You and your sales manager may feel more comfortable, but it's not productive. Go to an event with a plan to divide and conquer. Your attendance will now be worth your valuable time. I also would recommend the two of you choose different events. Spreading yourselves out allows you to cover more ground.

Regarding whether your time is worth attending or not, I strongly believe networking and building relationships is very important—whether you're doing it for business development or for strategic reasons.

Most of my networking is about finding more resources to bring to my peer advisory group of CEOs. It's not to generate more business for me, but for me to find more services or revenue channels for my CEOs. During this process, I've been able to meet some very interesting people who have encouraged me to keep my pulse on what's new in business development. I personally believe face-to-face networking is worth my time. You may want to test these practices out and assess your results.

Hosting an Event

Question:

My question relates to being the host rather than a guest of an event. Sometimes, it's difficult for the host to predict the turnout for an event. Many times, the people who don't attend are the ones most sought after by attendees. Given that you have a solid networking strategy in place, what can be done to avoid disconnects or loss due to the absence of an anticipated person at a networking event?

Devanand S. Deshmukh
BNI Executive Director – Pimpri Chinchwad Region
www.bni-pimprichinchwad.in | bni.com

Answer:

Instead of focusing on who the people are who are coming, gear up for a productive networking event for all involved. My emphasis would be on the strategy or premise that you are providing a great event regardless of who shows up.

How do you do that? First, make sure people will enjoy the event. Choose a desirable venue, one that makes it easy for people to mingle—offering food and beverages is always a plus, but not necessary. This way people don't specifically come for any particular person—they come for the event. Focus on increasing the numbers of individuals and the connections they will be able to make. It now becomes more about connecting. The success of the event is not dependent on any one person. Avoid advertising or even mentioning a particular person may attend. This way you don't set up your participants for disappointment. This reduces pressure for everyone and makes people feel like they are part of the crowd.

Ice Breakers

Question:

Attending events at which you do not know anyone or only one person can be difficult. What are some good ice-breaker questions / topics to ask a total stranger at the networking event that will lead to a conversation and not just a "yes" or "no" answer?

Kimberley Best Robidoux
Senior Attorney
Maggio Kattar Nahajzer + Alexander, P.C.
http://www.maggio-kattar.com/

Answer:

I love this question and am happy to share my answer. You're smart to pre-think before you enter conversations with people. You want to make sure you are saying something a little different from everyone else. You will be more productive and memorable in this way.

After you have exchanged names, ask the person to talk about themselves, specifically something that gets them excited. Try: "What's the most exciting thing(s) you're looking forward to this year?" This broad question opens up many different topics about a person, their life and livelihood. In addition, it allows them to light up about upcoming events and gives you some personal information. Information you can use in the future to show them you personally care about them. For example, "How is your new baby niece?" "Did you see the whales on your cruise?" "How was your business trip to Italy?" All are questions based on your initial conversation.

If a year seems too long, you might adjust your opening to: "What are you looking forward to this weekend?" or "When you're not working, what do you do for fun?" or "What are your favorite local places to eat?"

These types of questions jumpstart talking points and immediately shift the conversation away from what people are used to. It's a great way to get started.

PERSONALITIES

Genuine Care

Question:

I've been hearing more and more that the terminology "selling" is evolving into "relationship marketing." How can I approach *and* show someone (who I have yet to personally meet) that I would like to help them reach their desired goal? How would you suggest I encourage an individual to join in an online relationship / partnership who I haven't met?

Barry A. Bagus
Director
EMPTECH
www.emptech.com

Answer:

Whenever you meet someone for the first time, whether it's online or in person, it is the beginning of a relationship. You want to convey that you sincerely wish to help him or her. Being of value to another individual has a lot to do with your interactions.

For example, when I connect with someone on LinkedIn, as soon as they accept my invitation or as soon as I accept their invitation—I send people a message thanking them for connecting with me. I also offer them a gift of "Quoteactions." The quotes are a token that's unrelated to my business. They are something unique that communicates I value the relationship. With all my interactions, I start out by giving.

Nurturing a relationship has to do with your demeanor and approach. You can help a person by giving them a LinkedIn testimonial. Many individuals have given me testimonials that attest to the fact I value relationships, am an expert and giver. Through testimonials others do the talking for me. It's a subtle approach. You build more ethos through others' words than your own when it comes to self-promotion.

Start by ensuring you come across as someone who's genuinely interested in helping. Actionable help—not just telling people you want to help. I often encourage people to reach out to those "around" them and make their LinkedIn connections available. Or say, "Hey, listen,

I'll be happy to introduce you to people who may be able to help you reach your goals."

Another way you can show you sincerely care is by telling them, "Feel free to look over my connections and see if there's anyone you'd like to meet. I'd be happy to facilitate an introduction."

In the book I talk about some of the other "plays" you can use. One being sending people relevant content that communicates you are indeed a person who values relationships. Your contacts will see from your actions that you're interested in a partnership or relationship—you're not just talking or selling your services.

Introverts

Question:

Over the last 20 years of career coaching, I have frequently heard —"I am an introvert," or "I think networking is cheesy, and I am not one to 'work a room' full of strangers. Are there other ways to network for a job?"

Danielle M. Dayries
Founder/Career Coach
DMD & Associates, Inc. Outplacement & Career Consulting Firm
www.dmdcareerconsulting.com

Answer:

Being an introvert may be an advantage when it comes to networking as there's no rule about how you need to be gregarious to succeed in networking. You specifically asked about being an introvert who is looking for a job and also about job searching individuals who think networking is cheesy. In both cases, networking for a job is about finding people who can introduce you or open doors for you.

By being proactive and finding out who can open doors, you can find the exact connection or link you need. For example, my daughter is looking for a job for the summer. She put in her application at a local restaurant. I encouraged her to ask around to see if anyone knows anyone who works there or who has a relationship to the restaurant.

Sure enough, she found out that the father of one of her friends is an investor in the business. Furthermore, I found out I'm connected to someone who knows this person. I asked if they would be willing to put in a word for her. They said gladly. This is perfect example of job search networking in regard to my own daughter, who is a relative introvert.

I have found that people are willing to help on the condition you make it easy for them and provided that the help is commensurate to the level of relationship. It's kind of like asking a stranger at Disneyland, "Excuse me, can you help me out?" They will say, "What do you need?" You say, "Would you mind snapping a picture of my friend and I?" Most people will gladly assist you.

But if you were to ask that same stranger for $500 because you needed to buy a ticket home, they most likely will tell you to go take a hike. The level of the ask is not commensurate to your relationship. Networking is about connections. It's about finding the path from the people who you know to the people who you want to meet.

Being an introvert can be helpful because you are prone to listen and observe before you speak. Moreover, a person can feel more comfortable and actually find out a trove of information using online tools like LinkedIn. Behind their tablet or laptop, an introvert can find out what company he or she wants to work for, do a search for that company for a LinkedIn connection, and find out if they know anyone—either a first-degree or second-degree connection who already works there. Then they can ask for an introduction or other assistance. I truly don't think it matters whether you're extroverted or introverted. Both personality types can be very effective in networking.

To summarize, the best way to network for a job is to identify the business that has the job(s) that you want. Find out who is connected. Use online tools like LinkedIn to find these connections and then ask people for an introduction. It's a simple matter of asking.

Uncomfortable with Introductions

Question:

Like many people, I do well in a networking event where there are some people I know. But in a large group of people, I just don't feel comfortable introducing myself or inserting myself into a conversation. What should I do?

M. Erik Mueller
President and CEO
Grasp Technologies, Inc.
www.grasptech.com

Answer:

Believe it or not, this is a common concern for most people, myself included. Here's something that may be of help to you: view the event as an opportunity for you to play an ambassador. Imagine you are a host, and your job is to introduce people to one another.

Simply start conversations or get involved for the purpose of not necessarily finding people who will benefit you directly, but for finding people within the event or group who you can actually direct to one another. This takes some of the pressure off you and instantly makes you a helpful guy. For example, if you find out that somebody you're talking to is in biotech and later during the event, you meet somebody else who's in the same field you can say, "You know what?

There's someone here I believe you should meet because I think the two of you would benefit."

If you go to events with this mindset, it makes life significantly easier. It provides you with the opportunity to start conversations. I've found this approach positively affects your body. You are more likely to have an open, rather than closed, stance. Say there's two people talking to each other and their body language is closed. You can infer that they might be in an intense one-on-one discussion. But, when you are an ambassador, you stand more side-by-side people, encouraging introductions and openness.

We also have to remember that most people go to networking events for the same purpose: they want to meet people who can potentially benefit them and/or their businesses. That's what they are there to do! Remember, you are entering with a friendly mission—an introduction ambassador. As you're walking around, if you hear conversations, or if you see that there's more than two people talking to one another as a group, make eye contact. If you get a nod or an inviting gesture, come in with a smile and a simple "Hi, my name is Erik." And let them reply. You don't have to force the conversation but have a few ideas ready to contribute.

These tactics can help you be more comfortable getting into the conversation, which I certainly understand can be one of the most difficult steps we face in networking.

Etiquette

Question:

I network to build relationships to grow my business. I find as an Event Planner everyone wants to know how to get on "my list" instead of getting to know me. Can you touch on proper networking etiquette? In my case I don't have a "preferred vendor list." I focus on what my clients' needs are. At events I get business cards presented to me just to "have them" from people who don't even bother to take any time to get to know me. How do you deal with this?

Marie T. Rios
Event Producer/Planner
MTR Event Design
www.MTREventDesign.com

Answer:

The fact of the matter is that what you're describing is one of the mistakes that people make when they are networking—they make it all about themselves rather than focusing on building relationships. When someone comes up to you and asks how to get on your vendor list—instead of getting to know you—they are making a big mistake.

On your end, the proper etiquette is to tell them the truth: "I don't actually keep a preferred vendor list. I refer people with whom I build relationships and whose services fit my clients' needs."

From your perspective, when you're looking to connect with people, the etiquette is all about offering value. It's about building relationships with the people you're connecting with—otherwise those people will feel the same way you do, which is a total turnoff.

When you see they're self-centered, you may choose not to save their information in your database. Personally, I might just go ahead and send them an invitation to connect on LinkedIn as a second chance—giving them the benefit of the doubt so-to-speak. If they accept, I send them an invitation to receive my "QuoteActions" and see what happens.

NETWORK ORGANIZATION

Promoting Your Company

Question:

What is the best technique or way to build your network?

Karen Sachs
Prolific Artist, Facilitator, Workshop Leader & Coach
Paint Your Essence
https://paintyouressence.com/

Answer:

As far as the best technique to build your network, this may sound a bit cliché, but it is—one person at a time. Think about it this way: meet one person per week who could potentially impact your company in a beneficial way, that's about 50 people in a year. Do that for five or ten years, and you have 250 to 500 people. Slow and steady wins the race.

This formula applies to networking. Be strategic about how you go about networking. This will allow you to identify who are the best people—who know the people who can introduce you to the people that either will become your clients or a valued referral source. Let's say your target market is brides. While it would be nice to meet brides, better referral sources would be getting introductions to wedding planners, caterers, wedding photographers, etc.

Why? Because wedding planners know a ton of brides at any given time. Furthermore, they can introduce you to the bride-to-be. Think strategically about who the people are who work with your ideal clients. Then look to build relationships with these connections first, allowing yourself to expand your contact sphere circle out to caterers and photographers. Remember, give them added value, so they get to know, like and trust you. When they need someone with your services, you will be top-of-mind.

Being on people's radar is essentially what builds your network. Stay strategic and don't go after the end users. Go after the people who can introduce you to the end users. The quality and quantity of networking over time will increase tenfold. Voila, you have your network!

Networking Referrals
Questions:

Assuming a business owner is established in business over five years and adept at networking.

1. Is there a formula you recommend with regards to how many networking events one should attend per month?
2. Can you recommend the number of networking groups one should be a member of?
3. How do you balance out distribution of referrals when you network locally with more than one professional from the same industry?
4. If you could only choose one method of networking, would it be: (1) online; (2) in person; (3) a variety of meetups and mixers; or (4) being a member of a networking group that meets regularly?

Thomas J. Nelson, Realtor®
RCS-D, CRS, CDPE, ePro, Military Specialist
CA DRE# 01261476
Big Block Realty - San Diego
www.ThomasJNelsonRealtor.com

Answer Question 1:

There is no formula for determining how many events to attend per month. It depends on your objectives, and how many referrals you need.

First, you'll have to weigh in on the amount of time you're willing to devote to networking activities. Face-to-face networking takes quite a bit of time. I would say on average about three hours per event. You need to balance the amount of time that you spend at these events to see how many of these you can attend.

When you are first starting, you've got to go to as many as you can. With five years into your business, I would recommend adding LinkedIn activities to your strategy. You will get more bang for your buck if you combine the online with face-to-face networking. You can replace one face-to-face networking event with spending three hours a week on LinkedIn.

Next, determine your objectives and the volume you need. More quantity doesn't necessarily lead to more referrals. Consider what your objectives are in terms of the number of referrals you need—correlate how many relationships you think you can build. Average out how long it takes you to meet and connect with someone at an event. With this information, assess how effective and efficient those three hours will be for you. Based on that, come up with a personalized plan.

Answer to Question 2:

How many networking groups should you be a member of? I recommend you have three different types of groups. One of them, I refer to as a hard networking group. These are groups that meet every week or once every month. You certainly need to be part of a hard networking group. I was a member of BNI – Business Network

International for more than 15 years. Meetings were once a week. Currently I belong to a hard networking group, called ProVisors, meetings are once a month.

Second, you should be part of a service organization, like Kiwanis, Rotary, Soroptimist, etc. People bring a different mentality to non-profit, community involvement organizations. The relationships you build through your service networking group take on a different flavor.

Third, choose an organization that allows you to be more casual. Think of meet ups, chamber of commerce lunches, and evening mixers. You might attend these bi-monthly or quarterly. Categorize them as a large networking group.

A good rule of thumb is to attend these three types of networking organizations. They are very different in nature. You'll meet different people without much duplication. Check your schedule and see which ones have priority meetings and events. Then build your schedule to incorporate the other ones accordingly.

Answer to Question 3:

How do you balance distribution of referrals when you network with more than one professional from the same industry locally? First of all, I don't believe that you need to either balance or give everybody referrals. One of the ways you can address this scenario is to have the ability to give someone names of a number of professionals. Give people three names, saying, "I know these three people, all of whom I think can help you."

Another option for you is to talk to three professionals to see which one you feel more comfortable referring business. The other way is—I try to reciprocate more with people who have given me referrals / business or have been helpful. They take priority.

If somebody asks me why I gave one referral over another, or why I didn't provide their name, I tell them honestly that I carefully choose my referrals for each person. I let them know that I have given their name out, yet if the person doesn't call them, there is not much more I can do.

Remember, you can also offer people who refer business to you something other than referrals, something of equal value as a way of reciprocation.

Answer to Question 4:

If you could only choose one method of networking, what would it be? Oh tough question! I don't see why you would have to limit your methods. I do believe that online (in particular LinkedIn) and face-to-face is the best mix.

A percentage of your time should be devoted to the online component. I recommend Refer.com and LinkedIn. And a percentage of your face-to-face networking needs to be devoted to actual face-to-face connections. I think if you're only going to do one of the networking groups, I highly suggest being a member of a hard contact group. Both BNI and ProVisors are examples of organizations where you go deeper into your connections and the relationships with people.

To summarize, think through your strategy and commit to it. Two out of three networking groups are better than just going around to random events. Your commitment allows you to focus and build a base.

Invitation Influx

Question:

Having been very active in referral marketing with BNI and the Referral® Institute for 20 years, I find it hard to accept invitations from online social media applications. It seems a new one launches every time you turn around. Any advice on how I can strategically add this aspect without wasting a lot of valuable time?

Christopher C. Pennock
Vice President
Calender-Robinson Co., Inc.

Answer:

The question I ask people when this issue comes up is: "Are you thinking about these people like you would if you had met them at a networking event?" Let's say you go to an industry trade show or a big chamber of commerce event, would you talk to someone who's a stranger? Hopefully, the answer is always 'yes.' I would because that's why we're both there—to network. Online networking opportunities can save you time.

I see an invitation to connect, even from someone I don't know, as the beginning of a conversation. Avoid trying to gauge the intent of the person. Generally, you can't tell who is serious about networking from those with ulterior motives. I give people the benefit of the doubt. To save time, I accept their invitation, and I immediately start a conversation in a pointed direction.

I send individuals a message stating that I just sent them an invitation to connect on LinkedIn. You can see the message once they accept it. Let the conversation and connections build from here, assessing along the way if the relationship is mutually beneficial. You can always disconnect with people if they don't have any interest in networking with you or they try to sell or spam you.

I want to note here that I've been surprised over the years at how people who seemingly have no reason whatsoever for me to be connected with—have proven to be valuable either to me personally and/or to someone in my network. My strategy is to send a pre-written or template message, spending very little time here, to see if they respond favorably to my reply invitation or my reply conversation. Based on that, I pick and choose which ones I want to keep connected to. It really doesn't take much time, and you maintain control while potentially finding gems of connections who may pay future dividends. Send me an invitation to connect on LinkedIn, and you'll see the exact message I send out.

Go to https://www.linkedin.com/in/ritzkowich/

If this still seems too time consuming, this could be a job for a personal assistant. If you do not currently work with a personal assistant, you can easily hire somebody to be able to do this type of task efficiently and inexpensively.

LinkedIn Profile

Questions:

1. Are LinkedIn profiles becoming a replacement for resumes?
2. How many connections do I need to have "at the very least?" A recruiter told me at least 250, or I'm not viewed as credible.
3. Even if I don't know someone personally, when is it okay to accept their request to connect?

Timi Gleason
Strategy Coach
Executive Goals

Answer to Question 1:

Are LinkedIn profiles becoming replacement for resumes? LinkedIn profiles are a key component when people are looking for jobs. In fact, I recommend people view their LinkedIn profile more as a personal sales page—than a resume. Through your profile, you are selling yourself. And, you must do it in a way that sells on LinkedIn. From this perspective, it does not replace your resume.

In addition, people who want to do business with you go to LinkedIn to see your credentials, experience, awards, and testimonials. It can make the difference between getting a new account or signing up a new customer. Your profile supplements your company website, as it tells your story.

Answer to Question 2:

How many connections do I need to have at the very least? I recommend that people have at least 500 connections on LinkedIn. For people who are active on LinkedIn, that is a benchmark, but more importantly, as you have more connections, your networking reach increases. There are different reasons for people to be connected—not all of them need to be close or immediate connections.

Answer to Question 3:

Even if I don't know someone personally, when is it okay to accept a request to connect? Treat this like you would at networking events: would you ever speak to someone that you don't know at a networking event? Typically, the response is always 'yes.' As far as I'm concerned, a LinkedIn connection is the beginning of a conversation with a stranger—with many becoming clients, prospects, friends, and partners.

Business Cards

Question:

What do I do with all these business cards I keep collecting at networking events?

Daniel Rubenstein
www.ALLinEntry.com

Answer:

When I get a business card, I send the person an invitation to connect on LinkedIn. From there I start my process, and it's a pretty effective one. With LinkedIn, you have the individual's contact information, so you don't need the card. If they respond, you can see what happens next and what kind of conversations develop.

In conjunction with LinkedIn, I recommend people use an online database management service. A .csv file of your contacts makes it easy to send out email newsletters through Mail Chimp or Constant Contact. Remember, staying in touch keeps you top-of-mind, so when they are ready to buy, they think of you.

BUSINESS MANAGEMENT IN NETWORKING

Networking to Cash

Question:

Building a network is a long-term process, which we know has inherent value. Still, how does one go from networking to converting the time and effort into $$$?

Brian Blacher
COO
Workout Bar
www.linkedin.com/in/brianblacher

Answer:

Let's talk about the conversion to dollars. First, I'm not sure if what you're measuring is the ROI from networking, or more specifically, you are curious about how networking leads to business. Both are valid questions.

Networking is a tool that provides the shortest route from the people you know to the people you want to meet. It's easier to get introductions from going through people you know than doing it yourself. People think of networking as going to events and meeting people that they *won't* do business with. I see networking much more broadly. Sure, you'll meet people that you will or won't do business with—but networking overall is a means to add value to your connections through introductions. By building relationships, establishing goodwill, and planting seeds, people are much more likely to help you when the time is right. It's human nature. Your connections may be willing to help you out by facilitating introductions to the people who you want to meet. *That's* how you convert it into money.

Marketing Strategy

Question:

What do you consider to be the top marketing strategies professional service firms should employ to generate quality referrals?

Larry B. Comp
President
LTC Performance Strategies, Inc.
www.LTCPerformance.com

Answer:

Top marketing strategies to generate referrals on an ongoing basis require a variety of different approaches because timing is so important.

Since you want to make it easy for people to give you referrals, simplicity is of utmost importance. Be sure they know what your specialization is, and what sets you apart from others in your industry. Be sure to establish reasons for them to know, like and trust you. Do they understand you will reciprocate? The above is the foundation for why people will give you referrals and, more importantly, keep giving you referrals.

Establish a systematic approach for getting and giving referrals. It will provide you with long-term success.

Ask yourself what you can do to generate a feeling of reciprocity. Keep in mind reciprocity goes beyond the service(s) you offer. If you go out of your way for people, if you genuinely care for them, and if you show that they matter to you, they are much more likely to feel a mutual sense of reciprocity—not to mention remember you. And when you do ask for their help, it becomes easier. They'll think of you first and feel like doing whatever they can to help you out. Networking is all about farming not hunting. Plant seeds today to grow your business tomorrow.

Employ both building and visibility plays. Building plays are when you first meet people: what can you do to start nurturing the relationship once you've met them? What can you do to stay top-of-mind? When the need for your service(s) arises, will they think of you? This is a key component in getting referred. What are some of the ways you increase the human connection and the value that you bring to them—not only as a service provider, but as another human being who authentically cares about them?

When you do all these things, the odds that people will generate quality referrals for you increases exponentially. Hopefully, this will whet your appetite to get out there and use these strategies for success.

Publicity

Question:

My company, Productive Learning, can sponsor our local chamber of commerce and other networking gatherings by hosting their events at our workshop location. Is this a good idea for general publicity? If so, should I ask that we be mentioned or anything else?

Lindon A. Crow
President
Productive Learning
www.ProductiveLearning.com

Answer:

The short answer is 'yes.' This opportunity is a great idea for generating goodwill with the chamber and other organizations. With the extra bonus being that when people come into your facility to attend events, they get exposed to your marketing materials—handouts, promotional signs on the walls, upcoming workshop schedules etc. It also gives your staff the chance to chat with the attendees—building rapport and ramping up interest in your company. It also alerts other organizations that your facility is available for events.

I do think it's okay to ask to be recognized during the function as an event sponsor and the hosting facility. For example, you could propose to the event planner that a mention of your hosting be made during the event and/or you be given an opportunity to speak for a minute or two about Productive Learning. Even if they decline publicizing your company, hosting the event can be a big positive as far as business exposure.

If you want to be more quid pro quo, when asked to use your space, you can say, "Yes, we'll provide our facility in exchange for x, y, and z. It all depends on whether you want to treat this opportunity as a chance for cash / trade or as great PR. Think of it as making a deposit into the goodwill bank, with no strings attached for the organization.

From a networking perspective I think the former might be more appropriate than the latter when you are asked for help, but I can see both options working. Maybe try both. Then compare the before, during and after results, and I think you'll be pleasantly surprised.

Charity Balance

Question:

ZaneCO Homes belongs to the HBA (Housing and Building Association) and the HBA Cares. Each does charity work in the community. It seems the more meetings we attend and more events we help with—the more we are asked to do. At some point, the time and effort become difficult to balance. It's tough to measure the good it does for the business as well as the community. What are your thoughts on how to balance and measure the results as they impact sales *and* our community?

Zane Wilkerson
CSDO - Chief Sales Development Officer
ZaneCO Homes

Answer:

My thoughts on measuring your networking results is that it's part art and part science. Most of the time you will not see a direct correlation for your return on investment. I recommend you start with the end results in mind and work backwards.

Budget a certain amount of time that you are willing to invest in this type of networking. Write down whatever it is going to be. Will it be one hour a month, three or 10 hours a month? That's your limit. It's up to you to put the limitations in place and to use this as a baseline. Now focus on doing what you can within the timeframe. Ask yourself what the best avenues are for you to take to maximize your exposure while contributing to the community. Remember this is another way to build relationships with people while encouraging a sense of reciprocity.

Only you will realize when you have reached your time and money limits. People will continue to request your time and resources. You need to speak up and say, "I'm sorry, but we can't contribute at this stage" or "I'm already doing x, y, and z. I will have to complete or stop doing x or y before I have time to add your new request."

Best case scenario is that you now have a plan in place to help you manage your time, efforts and financial outlay. This will help you work with the organizations in a positive manner. Be sure to track the key people you network with in your database. Connect with them on LinkedIn. Nurture your relationships as you would with your other business development activities. If referrals come in through your interactions, you'll have seen how you can turn lemons into lemonade.

LinkedIn Leads

Question:

I am being approached by companies claiming they can access LinkedIn for us and/or help us find leads for our services and products. How can I tell if they can do what they say they can do? And, regarding LinkedIn, what can I realistically expect for potential clients by tapping into this resource?

R. J. Kelly, ChFC, CLU, IAR, CAP, RICP, MSFS
Founder & Chief Visionary Officer
Wealth Legacy Group®, Inc.
www.wealthlegacygroup.com

Answer:

Let's first establish that this process is called lead generation versus networking. You can generate these leads yourself on LinkedIn.

However, for some, paying for this service might be a cost-effective alternative. There are certainly some companies more reputable than others.

You will need to have seriously vetted the companies that approach you. References are key. Be sure to ask for names and contact information of people in similar industries you can talk to about the services and results they have achieved by working with XYZ Company. Once you've found a solid, reputable company, what can you expect from their work? Ask for a detailed proposal of their services and how you will be able to use the results / connections they promise you.

I explain to people LinkedIn is no different than face-to-face networking when it comes to building relationships. What LinkedIn does is—it gives you the option of finding more people faster in someone's network. Basically, you and I might know each other quite well, but I don't know all the people who you know. If I were to ask you, "Hey, RJ, do you know any CEOs who might be interested in joining my Vistage group?" You may say, "Maybe. Let me get back to you." While I'm waiting for you to reply, I can do a search on your LinkedIn account.

Your account would show me who you're connected to, and I could quickly come up with names of people. I then can be proactive and ask you, "What about this guy or what about that guy?" This makes the process much easier for you. And there are people who you may not have thought about or may have forgotten about. You could easily decipher who would be a good fit for me and then help facilitate an introduction to that person.

What you can expect from LinkedIn is the ability to get and give more referrals to other people. Your LinkedIn activities generate goodwill. Because of generating goodwill, you start the process of reciprocity. To me, that is LinkedIn's greatest value.

Do you have question?

Please email me your question(s) at rick@rickitzkowich.com

NOW WHAT?

You've read the playbook. Now what?

If you're like most successful people, you have a stash of business books on your print and digital shelves. Since many are concept books, the information shared gets assimilated in your brain bank to draw upon as needed. With *The Referral Playbook* you specifically were attracted to the fact that it was going to be a "how to" or "guide."

General Creighton Williams Abrams Jr. is credited with the proverb, "When eating an elephant take one bite at a time." Abrams was a United States Army general who commanded military operations during the Vietnam War.

Yes, we've all heard the saying, and it's the best advice I can give you to put the ideas and resources of this book to work for you. I would suggest your first bite includes committing four weeks, one to two hours per week, to implement the strategies covered in the checklists: Week 1 - Mindset to Win; Week 2 - Equipment to Win; Week 3 - Offline Places to Win; and Week 4 - Online Places to Win. By doing the action items in the lists, you are revving up your game. You will establish a strong foundation to add the additional high-power, high-touch resources I have included.

In addition, I like to recommend accountability partners. If you work with a business coach or mentor, let them know you are implementing *The Referral Playbook* and would like to include the action items in your plan. Or, you can find a member of your exec or sales team to pair up with to implement the strategies and tactics together.

I discovered or created many of the resources included and have been working the tenets of the playbook for more than 10 years now. I have achieved a seven-figure income. Through workshops, videos, and coaching, I have shared what I've learned in bits and pieces — up until now! With the full-on playbook, you now have the knowledge, which equals power. Commit at least six months to the playbook action items, and I assure you that you will see dramatic results.

In addition, please visit my website https://www.rickitzkowich.com often to read articles, watch videos, and learn about my new books, products and services.

And remember, "Whether you think you can, or you can't . . . either way you're right." Henry Ford

In success,

Rich Itzkowich

Please pay it forward by taking the time to review *The Referral Playbook* on Amazon at this link https://amazon.com/dp/1942489595#customerReviews.

Thank you in advance for your help!

ABOUT THE AUTHOR

Rick Itzkowich (It's-ko-witch) aka Rick I – The LinkedIn Guy is a genuine people connector. He bridges the two worlds of face-to-face networking and online networking. He understands and practices networking like few others do.

As an official member of the **Forbes Coaches Council** and recognized **Forbes *CommunityVoice*™** Contributor, Rick is a successful serial entrepreneur who creates turnkey products that meet today's demand for tools to increase your business.

Rick speaks to a diverse group of sales, networking, and professional organizations. He is a regular SCORE® workshop presenter. Internationally, Rick's LinkedIn presentation earned the Best Speaker Award at the "You Learn Twit Face" international social media conference held in Dubai.

His "Yikes! Workshop" has been presented around the globe.

Award-Winning Expertise

As a Vistage Chair, his passion is helping CEOs exponentially increase their companies' growth rates while improving their personal lives by working fewer hours. As the CEO of a successful manufacturing company and former business partner of a professional development firm, Rick has logged more than 30,000 hours of corporate facilitation.

On A Personal Note

Rick was born and raised in Mexico City. He speaks five languages and has traveled to forty-three countries while facilitating learning vacations. He currently plays on a nationally ranked tournament baseball team.

Contact

Rick Itzkowich
Vistage Chair, Entrepreneur, Speaker & Author
(858) 456-7653

rick@rickitzkowich.com
www.rickitzkowich.com
www.thereferralplaybook.com

LinkedIn

www.linkedin.com/in/ritzkowich

Facebook

https://www.facebook.com/thereferralplaybook

Twitter

https://twitter.com/TheLinkedinGuy

PRODUCTS & SERVICES

As the founder of 501 Connections, Inc. and a San Diego Vistage Chair, Rick is a genuine twenty-first century people connector and game changer. He understands and practices networking as few others do. As a successful entrepreneur, Rick creates turnkey products like QuoteActions, Link Power Now, Rock-IT! Referrals, and YIKES! Workshops.

QuoteActions Is an automated product using a web-based email delivery system. It's turnkey and maintenance-free. QuoteActions allows you to quickly start filling your sales pipeline, creating more revenue and profits. QuoteActions helps you turn your suspects into prospects, prospects into clients, and clients into raving fans.

Cost: $1 for the first month and $34.95/month or $359/year. Go to: https://www.getquoteactions.com

Rock-IT! Referrals

LinkedIn's powerful database combined with technology tools for screensharing, content shortcuts, and online calendar scheduling creates a maxed-out, cost-effective, time-saving way to quadruple the number of targeted referrals you get from people you know.

Get video tutorials, "how to" eBooks, and a template guide with resources.

Cost: $497

Go to http://ntwrk.biz/rockitreferrals

Link Power Now Coaching Tutorials

If you are you ready to triple the number of referrals you give and receive, and are not on LinkedIn, or if you haven't got a clue as to why it would be good for your business, or if you would like to know how to go about capitalizing on all LinkedIn has to offer—the Link Power Now Coaching Tutorials are your answer.

Cost: $39/month

Go to http://ntwrk.biz/linkpowercoaching

Yikes Workshop & Speaking Engagements

One of Rick's passions is to do live presentations. Malcolm Gladwell in his book *Outliers* states that the best way to achieve international stardom is to spend 10,000 hours honing your skills. Rick has spent more than 30,000 hours honing his speaking skills. His YIKES! Workshops have been presented around the globe.

To book Rick as a speaker, call (858) 456-7653 or email rick@rickitzkowich.com

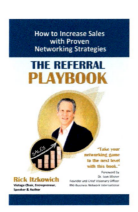

The Referral Playbook

To have access to updates to *The Referral Playbook* and/or to see videos, read articles, subscribe to podcasts, and more, go to:

https://www.thereferralplaybook.com

THANK YOU VERY MUCH!

I sincerely hope you will use the concepts I've shared in this book. One step, one day at a time. An hour here, an hour there. Please commit!

I know for a fact my clients, colleagues and peers have achieved success over the years by embracing the ideas I've coached and taught in my workshops. I knew the only way I would be able to reach the masses would be to write a book. Your review would be appreciated! Go to: https://amazon.com/dp/1942489595#customerReviews.

It's been a journey of close to a year from draft to publication. Why did it take so long? Because each step of the way special attention was paid to the content, images, formatting, links, marketing and more. Will I do it again? Time will tell.

But for now, I'd enjoy hearing from you about your experience using *The Referral Playbook* strategies and tactics. Go to my website https://www.rickitzkowich.com and click on the CONTACT button.

That's how we will start a conversation and begin our relationship. Yes?

Yours in Success!

Made in the USA
San Bernardino, CA
17 April 2019